Conversational AI with Rasa

Build, test, and deploy AI-powered, enterprise-grade
virtual assistants and chatbots

Xiaoquan Kong

Guan Wang

BIRMINGHAM—MUMBAI

Conversational AI with Rasa

Copyright © 2021 Packt Publishing

Publishing Product Manager: Devika Battike

Senior Editor: Mohammed Yusuf Imaratwale

Content Development Editor: Nazia Shaikh

Technical Editor: Devanshi Ayare

Copy Editor: Safis Editing

Project Coordinator: Aparna Ravikumar Nair

Proofreader: Safis Editing

Indexer: Sejal Dsilva

Production Designer: Joshua Misquitta

First published: October 2021

Production reference: 1260821

Published by Packt Publishing Ltd.

Livery Place

35 Livery Street

Birmingham

B3 2PB, UK.

ISBN 978-1-80107-705-7

www.packt.com

To my parents, for their unwavering devotion. To my wife, for her support behind the scenes. In addition, thanks to Google for providing the Google Cloud credits to support this work.

– Xiaoquan Kong

To my mom and dad. To my wife and kids. Thank you!

– Guan Wang

Foreword

Conversational AI combines ideas from linguistics, human-computer interaction, artificial intelligence, and machine learning to develop voice and chat assistants for a near-infinite set of use cases. Since 2016 there has been a surge in interest in this field, driven by the widespread adoption of mobile chat applications. The coronavirus pandemic accelerated this trend, with almost all one-on-one interactions becoming digital.

2016 was also the year Rasa was first released and we saw the first community contributions come in on GitHub. Open source communities live and die by their users and contributors, and this is doubly true for Rasa, where our global community builds assistants in hundreds of human languages. **Xiaoquan Kong** and **Guan Wang** have been leading members of our community for years and I am grateful for their many contributions. Not least Xiaoquan's efforts to ensure Rasa has robust support for building assistants in Mandarin. I've been eagerly awaiting the publication of this book.

Conversational AI with Rasa covers precisely the topics required to become proficient at building real-world applications with Rasa. Aside from covering the fundamentals of natural language understanding and dialogue management, the book emphasizes the real-world context of building great products. In the first chapter, you are challenged to think whether a conversational experience is even the right one to build. The book also covers the essential process of *Conversation-Driven Development*, without which many assistants get built but fail to serve their intended users. Additionally, readers are taught practical skills like debugging an assistant, writing tests, and deploying an assistant to production.

This book will be of great use for anyone starting out as a Rasa developer, and I'm sure many existing Rasa developers will discover things they didn't know.

Alan Nichol

Co-founder and CTO, Rasa

Contributors

About the authors

Xiaoquan Kong is a machine learning expert specializing in NLP applications. He has extensive experience of leading teams to build NLP platforms for several Fortune Global 500 companies. He is a Google Developer Expert in machine learning and has been actively involved in contributing to TensorFlow for many years. He also has actively contributed to the development of the Rasa framework since the early stages and became a Rasa Superhero in 2018. He manages the Rasa Chinese community and has also participated in the Chinese localization of TensorFlow documents as a technical reviewer.

Guan Wang is currently working on AI applications and research for the insurance industry. Prior to that, he worked as a machine learning researcher for several industry AI labs. He was raised and educated in mainland China and lived in Hong Kong for 10 years before relocating to Singapore in 2020. Guan holds BSc degrees in physics and computer science from Peking University, and an. MPhil degree in physics from HKUST. Guan is an active tech blogger and community contributor to open source projects including Rasa, receiving more than 10,000 stars for his own projects on GitHub.

About the reviewers

Harin Joshi's journey in chabot development started with an internship at ImpactGuru, India's fourth largest crowdfunding platform. There he developed two chatbots and a machine learning module. He was awarded Intern of the Month for this. Thereafter, he associated with the Co-learning Lounge AI community and developed a chatbot as educational content. Currently, he is working for the QuickGHY start-up as a chatbot developer.

I would like to thank my parents for always being there no matter what. Moreover, I am very grateful to have friends, who stood strong when I needed them at different stages of my life. And lastly, I would thank all the readers of this book: you are definitely going to learn a lot about Rasa and its functionalities.

Pratik Kotian is an conversational AI engineer with 5 years of experience in building conversational AI agents and designing products related to conversational design. He is working as a machine learning engineer (specializing in conversational AI) at Quantiphi, which is an AI company and recognized Google Partner. He has also worked with Packt on reviewing *The Tensorflow Workshop*.

I would like to thank my family and friends, who are always supportive and have always believed in me and my talents. It's because of them that I am doing well in my career and helping others to build great conversational bots.

Table of Contents

3

Rasa Core

Section 2: Rasa in Action

4

Handling Business Logic

8
Working Principles and Customization of Rasa

Section 3: Best Practices

9
Testing and Production Deployment

10

Conversation-Driven Development and Interactive Learning

11

Debugging, Optimization, and Community Ecosystem

Preface

The Rasa framework enables developers to create industrial-strength chatbots using state-of-the-art **natural language processing** (**NLP**) and machine learning technologies quickly, all in open source.

Conversational AI with Rasa starts by showing you how the two main components at the heart of Rasa work – Rasa NLU and Rasa Core. You'll then learn how to build, configure, train, and serve different types of chatbots from scratch by using the Rasa ecosystem. As you advance, you'll use form-based dialogue management, work with the response selector for chitchat and FAQ-like dialogues, make use of knowledge base actions to answer questions for dynamic queries, and more. Furthermore, you'll understand how to customize the Rasa framework, use conversation-driven development patterns and tools to develop chatbots, explore what your bot can do, and easily fix any mistakes it makes by using interactive learning. Finally, you'll get to grips with deploying the Rasa system to a production environment with high performance and high scalability and cover best practices for building an efficient and robust chat system.

By the end of this book, you'll be able to build and deploy your own chatbots using Rasa, addressing the common pain points encountered in the chatbot life cycle.

Who this book is for

This book is for NLP professionals and machine learning and deep learning practitioners who have knowledge of NLP and want to build chatbots with Rasa. Anyone with beginner-level knowledge of NLP and deep learning will be able to get the most out of the book.

What this book covers

Chapter 1, Introduction to Chatbots and the Rasa Framework, introduces all the fundamental knowledge pertaining to chatbots and the Rasa framework, including machine learning, NLP, chatbots, and Rasa Basic.

Chapter 2, Natural Language Understanding in Rasa, covers Rasa NLU's architecture, configuration methods, and how to train and infer.

Chapter 3, Rasa Core, introduces how to implement dialogue management in Rasa.

Chapter 4, Handling Business Logic, explains how Rasa gives developers great flexibility in handling different business logic. This chapter introduces how we can use these features to handle complex business logic more elegantly and efficiently.

Chapter 5, Working with Response Selector to Handle Chitchat and FAQs, explains how to define questions and their corresponding answers and how to configure Rasa to automatically identify the query and give the corresponding answer.

Chapter 6, Knowledge Base Actions to Handle Question Answering, describes how to create a knowledge base that will be used to answer questions. You will also learn to customize knowledge base actions, learn how referential resolution (mapping mention to object) works, and how to create your own knowledge base.

Chapter 7, Entity Roles and Groups for Complex Named Entity Recognition, explains how entity roles and entity groups solve the complex NER problem, and how to define training data, configure pipelines, and write stories for entity roles and entity groups.

Chapter 8, Working Principles and Customization of Rasa, introduces the working principles behind Rasa and how we can extend and customize Rasa.

Chapter 9, Testing and Production Deployment, explains how to test Rasa applications and how to deploy Rasa applications in production environments.

Chapter 10, Conversation-Driven Development and Interactive Learning, introduces conversation-driven development and Rasa X to develop chatbots more effectively. We will also introduce how to use interactive learning to quickly find and fix problems.

Chapter 11, Debugging, Optimization, and Community Ecosystem, explains how to debug and optimize Rasa applications. We will also introduce some tools to help developers build chatbots effectively.

To get the most out of this book

You will need a version of Rasa 2.x installed on your computer—the latest version if possible. All code examples have been tested using Rasa 2.8.1 on Ubuntu 20.04 LTS. However, they should work with future version releases, too.

Software/hardware covered in the book	Operating system requirements
Rasa	Windows, macOS, or Linux

You should install Rasa with the following command: `pip install rasa[transformers]`. This command will install the `transformers` library, which provides the components we need in the code.

You will also need to install the `pyowm` Python package to run the code present in *Chapter 4, Handling Business Logic*. You will also need to install Docker and the `neo4j` Python package 4.1 to run the code of the custom knowledge base part in *Chapter 6, Knowledge Base Actions to Handle Question Answering*.

If you are using the digital version of this book, we advise you to type the code yourself or access the code from the book's GitHub repository (a link is available in the next section).

The versions of Rasa change quickly, and the related knowledge base and documents are also rapidly updated. We recommend that you frequently read Rasa's documentation to understand the changes.

Download the example code files

You can download the example code files for this book from GitHub at `https://github.com/PacktPublishing/Conversational-AI-with-RASA`. If there's an update to the code, it will be updated in the GitHub repository.

We also have other code bundles from our rich catalog of books and videos available at `https://github.com/PacktPublishing/`. Check them out!

Download the color images

We also provide a PDF file that has color images of the screenshots and diagrams used in this book. You can download it here: `https://static.packt-cdn.com/downloads/9781801077057_ColorImages.pdf`.

Conventions used

There are a number of text conventions used throughout this book.

`Code in text`: Indicates code words in text, database table names, folder names, filenames, file extensions, pathnames, dummy URLs, user input, and Twitter handles. Here is an example: "The following example demonstrates post-mortem debugging using the `pdb` command."

A block of code is set as follows:

```
version: "2.0"
language: en
pipeline:
  - name: WhitespaceTokenizer
  - name: LanguageModelFeaturizer
```

When we wish to draw your attention to a particular part of a code block, the relevant lines or items are set in bold:

```
WebChat.default.init({
        selector: "#webchat",
        initPayload: "Hello",
```

Any command-line input or output is written as follows:

```
python -m pdb -c continue <XXX>/rasa/__main__.py train
```

Bold: Indicates a new term, an important word, or words that you see on screen. For instance, words in menus or dialog boxes appear in **bold**. Here is an example: "Click on the **Cancel** button."

Tips or important notes
Appear like this.

Get in touch

Feedback from our readers is always welcome.

General feedback: If you have questions about any aspect of this book, email us at customercare@packtpub.com and mention the book title in the subject of your message.

Errata: Although we have taken every care to ensure the accuracy of our content, mistakes do happen. If you have found a mistake in this book, we would be grateful if you would report this to us. Please visit www.packtpub.com/support/errata and fill in the form.

Piracy: If you come across any illegal copies of our works in any form on the internet, we would be grateful if you would provide us with the location address or website name. Please contact us at copyright@packt.com with a link to the material.

If you are interested in becoming an author: If there is a topic that you have expertise in and you are interested in either writing or contributing to a book, please visit `authors.packtpub.com`.

Share your thoughts

Once you've read *Conversational AI with Rasa*, we'd love to hear your thoughts! Scan the QR code below to go straight to the Amazon review page for this book and share your feedback.

`https://packt.link/r/1801077053`

Your review is important to us and the tech community and will help us make sure we're delivering excellent quality content.

Section 1: The Rasa Framework

In this section, you will learn about the core concepts of machine learning, natural language processing, dialogue systems, and Rasa. All these foundational concepts will prepare you for subsequent learning.

This section comprises the following chapters:

- *Chapter 1, Introduction to Chatbots and the Rasa Framework*
- *Chapter 2, Natural Language Understanding in Rasa*
- *Chapter 3, Rasa Core*

1

Introduction to Chatbots and the Rasa Framework

In this first chapter, we will introduce chatbots and the **Rasa** framework. Knowledge of these is important because they will be used in later chapters. We will split that fundamental knowledge into four pieces, of which the first three are **machine learning (ML)**, **natural language processing (NLP)**, and **chatbots**. This is the theory and concept part of the fundamentals. With these in place, you will know in theory how to build a chatbot.

The last piece is **Rasa basics**. We will introduce the key technology of this book: the Rasa framework and its basic usage.

In particular, we will cover the following topics:

- What is ML?
- Introduction to NLP
- Chatbot basics
- Introduction to the Rasa framework

Technical requirements

Rasa is a Python-based framework. To install it, you need a Python developer environment, which can be downloaded from `https://python.org/downloads/`. At the time of writing this chapter, Rasa only supports Python 3.6, 3.7, and 3.8, so please be careful to choose the correct Python version when you set up the developing environment.

You can find all the code for this chapter in the `ch01` directory of the GitHub repository, at `https://github.com/PacktPublishing/Conversational-AI-with-RASA`.

What is ML?

ML and **artificial intelligence (AI)** have almost become *buzzwords* in recent years. Everyone must have heard about AI in the news after AlphaGo from Google beat the best Go player in the world. There is no doubt that ML is now one of the most popular and advanced areas of research and applications. So, what exactly is ML?

Let's imagine that we are building an application to automatically recognize rock/paper/scissors based on video inputs from a camera. The hand gesture from the user will be recognized by the computer as one of rock/paper/scissors.

Let's look at the differences between ML and traditional programming in solving this problem.

In traditional programming, the working process usually goes like this:

1. **Software development**: Product managers and software engineers work together to understand business requirements and transform them into detailed business rules. Then, software engineers write the code to transform business rules into computer programs. This stage is shown as process **1** in the following diagram.

2. **Software usage**: Computer software transforms users' input to output. This stage is shown as process **2** in the following diagram:

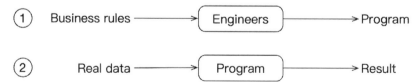

Figure 1.1 – Traditional programming working pattern

Let's go back to our rock/paper/scissors application. If we use a traditional programming methodology, it will be very difficult to recognize the position of hands and boundaries of the fingers, not to mention that even the same gesture can evolve into many different representations, including the position of the hand, different sizes and shapes of hands and fingers, different skin colors, and so on. In order to solve all these problems, the source code will be very cumbersome, the logic will become very complicated, and it will become almost impossible to maintain and update the solution. In reality, probably no one can accomplish their target with traditional programming methodology.

On the other hand, in ML, the working process usually follows this pattern:

1. **Software development**: The ML algorithm infers hidden business rules by learning from training data and encodes the business rules into models with lots of weight parameters. Process **1** in the following diagram shows the data flow.

2. **Software usage**: The model transforms users' input to output. In the following diagram, process **2** corresponds to this stage:

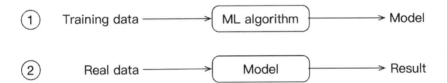

Figure 1.2 – Programming working pattern driven by ML

There are a few types of ML algorithms: **supervised learning (SL)**, **unsupervised learning (UL)**, and **reinforcement learning (RL)**. In NLP, the most useful and most common algorithms belong to SL, so let's focus on this learning algorithm.

Supervised learning (SL)

An SL algorithm builds a mathematical model of a set of data that contains both the inputs (x) and the expected outputs (y). The algorithm's input data is also known as training data, composed of a set of training examples. The SL algorithm learns a function or a mapping from inputs to outputs of training data. Such a function or mapping is called a model. A model can be used to predict outputs associated with new inputs.

The algorithm used for our rock/paper/scissors application is an SL algorithm. More specifically, this is a **classification task**. Classification is a task that requires algorithms to learn how to assign (limited) class labels to examples—for example, classifying emails as "spam" or "non-spam" is a classification task. More specifically, it divides data into two categories, so it is a **binary classification task**. The rock/paper/scissors application in this example divides the picture into three categories, so, to be more specific, it belongs to a **multi-class classification task**. The opposite of a classification task is a **regression task**, which predicts a continuous quantity output for each example—for example, predicting future house prices in a certain area is a regression task.

Our application's training data contains the data (the image) and a label (one of rock/paper/scissors), which are the **input and output** (**I/O**) of the SL algorithm. The data consists of many pictures. As the example in the following screenshot shows, each picture is simply a big matrix of pixel values for the algorithm to consume, and the label of the picture is rock or paper or scissors for the hand gesture in the picture:

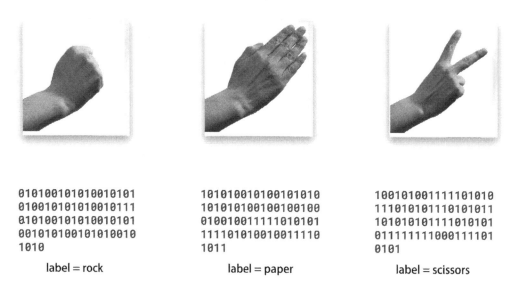

Figure 1.3 – Data and label

Now we understand what an SL algorithm is, in the next section, we will cover the general process of ML.

Stages of machine learning

There are three basic stages of applying ML algorithms: **training**, **inference**, and **evaluation**. Let's look at these stages in more detail here:

1. **Training stage**: The training stage is when the algorithms learn knowledge or business rules from training data. As shown in process **1** in *Figure 1.2*, the input of the training stage is training data, and the output of the training stage is the model.

2. **Inference stage**: The inference stage is when we use a model to compute the output label of a new input data. The input of this stage is the new input data without labels, and the output is the most likely label.

3. **Evaluation stage**: In a serious application, we always want to know how good a model is before we use it in production. This is a stage called **evaluation**. The evaluation stage will measure the model's performance in various ways and can help users to compare models.

In the next section, we will introduce how to measure model performance.

Performance metrics

In NLP, most problems can be viewed as classification problems. A key concept in classification performance is a confusion matrix, on which almost all other performance metrics are based.

A confusion matrix is a table of the model predictions versus the ground-truth labels.

Let me give you a specific example. Assume we are building a binary classification to classify whether an image is a cat image or not. When the image is a cat image, we call it a positive. Remember—we are building an application to detect cats, so a cat image is a positive result for our system, and if it is not a cat image (in our case, it's a dog image), we call it a negative. Our test data has 10 images. The real label of test data is listed as follows, where the cat image represents a cat and the dog image represents a dog:

Figure 1.4 – The real label of test data

The prediction result of our model is shown here:

Figure 1.5 – The prediction result of our model on test data

The confusion matrix of our case would look like this:

Actual class / Predicted class	Cat( )	Dog( )
Cat( )	4	2
Dog( )	1	3

Figure 1.6 – The confusion matrix of our case

In this confusion matrix, there are five cat images, and the model predicts that one of them is a dog. This is an error, and we call it a **false negative** (**FN**) because the model says it is a negative result, but that is actually incorrect. And in the five dog images, the model predicts that two of these are cats. This is another error, and we call it a **false positive** (**FP**) because the model says it is a positive result but it's actually incorrect. All correct predictions belong to one of two cases: cats-to-cats prediction, which we call a **true positive** (**TP**), and dogs-to-dogs prediction, which we call a **true negative** (**TN**).

So, the preceding confusion matrix can be viewed as an instance of the following abstract confusion matrix:

Actual class / Predicted class	Positive(P)	Negative(N)
Positive(P)	True Positive (TP)	False Positive (FP)
Negative(N)	False Negative (FN)	True Negative (TN)

Figure 1.7 – The confusion matrix in abstract terms

Many important performance metrics are derived from a confusion matrix. Here, we will introduce some of the most important ones, as follows:

- **Accuracy** (**ACC**):

$$ACC = \frac{TP + TN}{TN + TP + FN + FP}$$

- **Recall**:

$$recall = \frac{TP}{TP + FN}$$

- **Precision**:

$$precision = \frac{TP}{TP + NP}$$

- **F1 score**:

$$F1\ score = 2 \times \frac{recall + precision}{recall \times precision}$$

Among the preceding metrics, the F1 score is the combined advantage of recall and precision, so it is the most commonly used metric for now.

In the next section, we will talk about the root cause of poor performance (the performance metrics being low): overfitting and underfitting.

Overfitting and underfitting

Generally speaking, there are two types of errors found in ML models: **overfitting** and **underfitting**.

When a model performs poorly on the training data, we call it underfitting. Common reasons that can lead to underfitting include the following:

- The algorithm is too simple. It does not have enough power to capture the complexity of the training data. For algorithms based on neural networks, there are too few hidden layers.

- The network architecture or features used for training is not suitable for the task—for example, models based on **bag-of-words** (**BoW**) are not suitable for complex NLP tasks. In these tasks, the order of words is critical, but a BoW model completely discards this information.

- Training a model for too few **epochs** (a full training pass over the entire training data so that each example has been seen once) or at too low a **learning rate** (a scalar used to train a model via gradient descent, which can determine the degree of weight changes).

- Using a too-high **regularization rate** (a scale used to indicate the penalty degree on a model's complexity; the penalty can reduce the power of fitting) to train a model.

When a model performs very well on the training data but performs poorly on new data that it has never seen before, we call this overfitting. Overfitting means the algorithm has the ability to fit the training data well, but it does not generalize well to samples that are not in the training data. **Generalization** is the most important key feature of ML. It means that algorithms learn some key concepts from training data rather than just simply remembering them. When overfitting happens, it shows that the model is more likely to remember what it saw in training than learn from it, so it performs very well on the training data, but since it does not see the new data before and does not learn the concept well, it thus performs poorly on the new data. ML scientists have already developed various methods against overfitting, such as adding more training data, regularization, dropout, and stopping early.

In the next section, we will introduce TL, which is very useful when the training data is insufficient (this is a common situation).

Transfer learning (TL)

TL is a method where a model can use knowledge from another model for another task.

TL is popular in the chatbot domain. There are many reasons for this, and some of them are listed here:

- **TL needs less training data**: In a chatbot domain, there usually is not much training data. When using a traditional ML method to train a model, it usually does not perform well due to a lack of training data. With TL, we can achieve much better performance on the same amount of training data. The less data you have, the more performance increase you can get.
- **TL makes training faster**: TL only needs a few training epochs to fine-tune a model for a new task. Generally, it is much faster than the traditional ML method and makes the whole development process more efficient.

Now we understand what ML is, in the next section, we will cover the basics of NLP.

Introduction to Natural Language Processing (NLP)

NLP is a subfield of linguistics and ML, concerned with interactions between computers and humans via text or speech.

Let's start with a brief history of NLP.

Evolution of modern NLP

Before 2013, there was no unified method for NLP. This was because two problems had not been solved well.

The first problem relates to how we represent textual information during the computing process.

Time-series data such as voices can be represented as signals and waves. Image information gives pixel position and pixel value. However, there were no intuitive ways to digitalize text. There were some preliminary methods such as one-hot encoding to represent each word or phrase and use BoW to represent sentences and paragraphs, but it became quite obvious that this was not the perfect way to deal with this.

After one-hot encoding, the dimension of each vector will be the size of the entire vocabulary, with all 0 values except one value of 1, to represent the position of that word. Such sparse vectors waste a lot of space and, in the meantime, give no indication of the semantic meaning of the word itself—every pair of two different words will always be orthogonal to each other.

A **BoW** model simply counts the frequency of each word that appears in the text and ignores the dependency and order of the words in the context.

The second problem relates to how we can build models for text.

Traditional methods rely heavily on manually engineered features—for example, we use **Term Frequency-Inverse Document Frequency** (**TF-IDF**) to represent the importance of a word with respect to its frequency in both an article and a whole group of articles. We use topic modeling to inform us of the document theme and ratio of different themes for each article with respect to statistical information. We also use lots of linguistic information to manually engineer features.

Let's take an example from an open source tool called **IEPY** that is used for relation extraction. Here is a list of the engineered features of IEPY constructs for its relation extraction task:

- `number_of_tokens`
- `symbols_in_between`
- `in_same_sentence`
- `verbs_count`
- `verbs_count_in_between`
- `total_number_of_entities`

- `other_entities_in_between`
- `entity_distance`
- `entity_order`
- `bag_of_wordpos_bigrams_in_between`
- `bag_of_wordpos_in_between`
- `bag_of_word_bigrams_in_between`
- `bag_of_pos_in_between`
- `bag_of_words_in_between`
- `bag_of_wordpos_bigrams`
- `bag_of_wordpos`
- `bag_of_word_bigrams`
- `bag_of_pos`
- `bag_of_words`

After getting all those features, traditional methods use some traditional ML algorithms to build models. Let's take IEPY as an example again. It provides the following classification models:

- **Stochastic Gradient Descent (SGD)**
- **Nearest Neighbors (NN)**
- **Support Vector Classification (SVC)**
- **Random Forest (RF)**
- **Adaptive Boosting (AdaBoost)**

Traditional applications of NLP usually practice in a very similar way to that shown previously to solve real problems. We will see later that Rasa solves the **entity recognition (ER)** problem in a similar way. The advantage is that the training process can be really fast, and it requires less label data to train a working model. However, this also means that we need to spend a lot of time and effort manually engineering the features and tuning the models. It also does not work well for more complicated contexts.

In 2013, Tomas Mikolov published two research papers that introduced **Continuous BoW (CBOW)** and Skip-gram models. Soon after that, an open source tool called **word2vec** was released.

word2vec solves the main issue of our first problem in an elegant way, training itself through a shallow neural network with a large text corpus. By looking at the context for each of the words, the algorithm embeds the semantic meaning of each word into a strong and mysterious dense vector—a so-called word embedding. The vector is strong because the word embedding embeds the semantic meaning of the word itself so that we can even do operations such as *King - Man + Woman = Queen* that were unimaginable before with one-hot encoding. It is also mysterious because we still do not fully understand what it means for the value in each dimension of the word embedding.

This basically started a new era for NLP. With word2vec, the first step for NLP is normally to transform the words into word embeddings. With the help of word embeddings, the popular **deep learning** (**DL**) model in computer vision can also be applied to text. This is becoming popular and is gradually replacing traditional ML models. This solves our second question on how to model the texts. With word embeddings trained on a large corpus, being the input and **deep neural networks** (**DNNs**) as the model, this new pipeline became standard for many NLP tasks.

The invention of word2vec and word embeddings converted the one-hot encoding of words into vectors that are dense, mysterious, elegant, and expressive. It freed NLP from complicated and tedious linguistic features and pushed techniques such as DL to be applied to the NLP domain. This trend of representation learning has gone beyond NLP and into applications such as knowledge graphs (with graph embeddings) and recommendation systems (with user embeddings and item embeddings).

Although word2vec significantly improved NLP tasks, researchers soon discovered its shortcomings: in reality, the same word has different meanings in different contexts (for example, the word "bank" in "riverbank" and "financial bank" would have different embeddings), but the vector representation given by word2vec is static regardless of the context. So, why don't we give an embedding of a word based on the current context? This new technology is known as contextualized word embeddings. Among the early models that introduced contextualized word embeddings is the famous **Embeddings from Language Models** (**ELMo**). ELMo does not use fixed embeddings for each word but looks at the entire sentence before assigning embeddings to each word. It uses a bi-directional **long short-term memory** (**LSTM**) trained on a specific task to create these embeddings. LSTM is a special **recurrent neural network** (**RNN**) that can learn long-term dependencies (the large distance between the relevant information and the point where it is needed). It performs well on various problems and has become a core component of the NLP algorithm based on DL.

The **Transformer** (`https://arxiv.org/abs/1706.03762`) model was released in 2017, and it performed amazing results on machine translation tasks. Transformer does not use LSTM in architecture but instead uses a lot of **attention** mechanisms. An attention mechanism is a function that maps a query and a set of key-value pairs to an output. The output is computed as a weighted sum of the values, where the weight of each value is computed by a function of the query and the corresponding key of the value. Some NLP researchers believe that the attention mechanism used in Transformer is a better alternative to LSTM. They believe that the attention mechanism handles long-term dependencies better than LSTM and has very promising and broad application prospects. Transformer adopts an encoder-decoder structure in the architecture. The encoder and decoder are highly similar in structure but not the same in their function. The encoder is composed of a stack of N identical encoder layers. The decoder is also composed of a stack of N identical decoder layers. Both the encoder layer and the decoder layer use the attention mechanism as the core component.

The great success of Transformer has attracted the interest of many NLP scientists. They have developed more excellent models based on Transformer. Among these models, two are very famous and important: **Generative Pre-trained Transformer** (**GPT**) and **Bidirectional Encoder Representations from Transformers** (**BERT**). GPT is entirely composed of Transformer's decoder layer, while BERT is entirely composed of Transformer's encoder layer. The goal of GPT is to produce human-like text. So far, GPT has developed three versions—namely, GPT-1, GPT-2, and GPT-3. The quality of the text generated by GPT-3 is very high—very close to a human level. The goal of BERT is to provide a better language representation to help a wide range of downstream tasks (sentence-pair classification tasks, single-sentence classification tasks, **question-answering** (**QA**) tasks, single-sentence tagging tasks) achieve better results. That year, the BERT model achieved state of the art on various NLP tasks and greatly improved the existing industry's best record on many tasks. Now, BERT has derived a large family tree, among which the more well-known ones are XLNet, RoBERTa, ALBERT, ELECTRA, ERNIE, BERT-WWM, and DistilBERT.

We have now learned the evolution process of modern NLP. In the next section, we will discuss the different types of tasks in NLP.

Basic tasks of NLP

The highly efficient embedding representations of words, phrases, and sentences reduce the heavy workload on feature engineering and open the door for a series of downstream NLP applications.

If we consider texts as sequences and different kinds of labels as categories, then the basic tasks of NLP can be categorized into the following groups with regard to the I/O data structures:

- **From categories to sequences**: Examples include text generation and picture-caption generation.

- **From sequences to categories**: Examples include text classification, sentiment analysis, and relation extraction. If the goal of text classification is to classify text according to the intent of the text, this is an intent classification task. An intent classification task is one of two important parts of **natural language understanding** (**NLU**), which will be introduced in the next section. The common sequences-to-categories algorithms include TextCNN, TextRNN, Transformers, and their variants. Although different algorithms have different structures, in general, a sequences-to-categories algorithm extracts the semantics of the sequence (the text) into a vector and then classifies the vector into categories.

- **Synchronous sequence to sequence (Seq2Seq)**: Examples include tokenization, **part-of-speech** (**POS**) tagging, semantic role labeling, and **named ER** (**NER**). NER is another important part of NLU besides intention classification. The common synchronous Seq2Seq algorithms include **Conditional Random Fields** (**CRF**), **Bidirectional LSTM** (**BiLSTM**)-CRF, Transformers, and their variants. Although the various algorithms work differently, the most common and classic algorithms in production are based on sequence annotation—that is, each element in the sequence is classified one by one, and finally, the classification results of all elements are combined into another sequence.

- **Asynchronous Seq2Seq**: Examples include machine translation, automatic summarization, and keyboard input methods.

We will see that in building chatbots, the intention-recognition task is a sequence-to-category task, while ER is a synchronous Seq2Seq task. **Automatic speech recognition** (**ASR**) can be generally considered as a synchronous *sequence* (*voice signals*) to *sequence* (*text*) task, and so is **Text to Speech** (**TTS**), but from text-to-voice signals. **Dialogue management** (**DM**) can be generally considered as an *asynchronous sequence* (*conversation history*) to *category* (*next action*) task.

Let's talk more about chatbots.

Chatbot basics

A chatbot is a software system that is used to have a conversation with people via text or speech. Chatbots are used for various purposes, including customer service, enterprise operations, and healthcare. According to the different goals, chatbots have two main types: task-oriented bots and chitchat bots. Task-oriented bots have the goal of finishing specific tasks by interacting with people, such as booking a flight ticket for someone, while chitchat bots are more like human beings—their goal is to respond to users' messages smoothly, just as with chitchat between people.

A chatbot is a *diamond in the crown* for NLP. The application of a chatbot is challenging, and we typically do not find the same patterns being used everywhere, from both technology and business perspectives. Here, we try to clear the fog and introduce some common processes for developing task-oriented chatbots focusing on vertical domains. Open-domain chitchat chatbots are also very important and interesting, but they are not within the scope of this book.

In the next section, we will discuss the advantages of chatbots in the business domain.

Is a chatbot really necessary?

Before we deep dive into the technology, we should ask ourselves the following question after looking at client requirements: do we really need a chatbot?

If you go to McDonald's, you have probably seen the automatic order system. It has a big touchscreen with some big buttons and pictures. It supports multiple ways of payment and requires customers to go through only a few intuitive steps to buy the food they want. Nowadays, in many McDonald's outlets, we only have one or two employees at the counter that deal with customers using cash payments, and most of the customers are already quite used to the automatic order system.

This is an example of a **user interface** (**UI**) requirement that deals with single and clear customer goals and with a few intuitive steps. Similar kinds of examples are purchasing movie tickets, booking train or plane tickets, booking hotel rooms, and buying coffee or food. Although many of these are used especially in academic research as chatbot examples, we have to understand that a chatbot may not be the best choice compared to a big touchscreen and buttons with pictures.

The UI scenarios in which a chatbot has a certain advantage are listed here:

- Customer service in vertical domains where customers generate a large number of similar questions and requirements. Goals are clear or semi-clear, and customers potentially need help and guidance to understand their own needs.

- Customer service (chatbot) owns domain expert knowledge (for example, knowledge graph) and strong experience in answering questions (historical customer service conversational data) and can solve customer problems within minutes.

- If the chatbot cannot eventually solve the customer's problem, it should collect as much information as possible and switch to manual customer service with all that information.

In many scenarios, the 10 most frequently asked questions can already solve a majority of the general problems customers have. The advantage of using a chatbot is that it can automatically retrieve customer profiles, read instantly from a large volume of knowledge bases, perform multiple rounds of conversations, and quickly give personalized solutions according to user needs.

Some example scenarios in which a chatbot may have an advantage are listed here:

- Hospital reception or medical consulting

- Online shopping customer service

- After-sales service

- Investment consulting

- Bank services

We have already seen many chatbot applications in the preceding scenarios. However, there is still a long way to go for chatbot applications to work in real life.

In the next section, we will learn about the theoretical principles of chatbots.

Introduction to chatbot architecture

In the early days, chatbots were mainly based on templates and rules. An example is **AI Markup Language** (**AIML**). AIML is quite powerful. It can extract important information by rules from users' questions, and it can run scripts to get information through an external **application programming interface** (**API**) to enrich the answers. There is a chatbot called **Artificial Linguistic Internet Computer Entity** (**Alicebot**) that is based on AIML, and it contains more than 40,000 different kinds of data, which literally constructs a huge rule-based knowledge base.

An advantage of using rules is that we can achieve high precision. However, there is also an obvious disadvantage: there can be many alternative formats of the same questions, and the best rules will only be able to cover part of them. Take an example of a weather bot—a user can have hundreds of ways of asking about the weather. Also, it becomes very difficult to maintain it once we have more and more rules written in the system. Very easily, there can be contradicting rules, and many times, a change in business logic means we need to rewrite a good part of all the rules.

Another way to build a chatbot is to have a huge QA database. When a user question comes in, the system calculates the similarity between that question and all the questions in the database, chooses the most similar one, and gives the corresponding answer. There are many similar tasks in the competitions held by Zhihu and Quora. Those websites do not want users to raise many duplicated questions, so they will match the new questions to existing questions and alert users if there is a high chance of duplication. Techniques such as skip-thought that calculate sentence embeddings were invented to tackle this sentence-similarity problem.

Recently, the mainstream process for building a chatbot has become unified. It mainly consists of five different modules to build a chatbot, outlined as follows:

- ASR to convert user speech into text
- NLU to interpret user input
- DM to take decisions on the next action with respect to the current dialogue status
- **Natural-language generation** (**NLG**) to generate text-based responses to the user
- TTS to convert text output into voice

In this book, we mainly focus on NLU and DM.

Here, we briefly introduce each of the modules.

Automatic Speech Recognition (ASR)

ASR converts human speech into corresponding text. There are many open source and commercial solutions for ASR, but we are not covering them in this book.

Natural Language Understanding (NLU)

NLU interprets text-based user input. It recognizes the intent and the relevant entities from a user's input. The NLU module mainly classifies a user's question at the sentence level and gets the user's clear intent by intent classification. The NLU module also recognizes the key entities in the word level from a user's question and performs slot filling. For multi-domain dialogue systems, there is an additional task before the intent classification and NER—that is, domain classification. Domain classification is used to predict the domain (topic) users want to talk about—for example, is that user talking about the music domain (*"Play Michael Jackson's Billie Jean"*), the navigation domain (*"Navigate to Carrefour"*), or the radio domain (*"Turn on radio 106.6 FM"*)? Of course, this domain classification is unnecessary for single-domain dialogue systems that are focused on only one domain. Since the Rasa framework is designed for single-domain dialogue systems, it does not include the domain classification feature. In this book, we will focus on how to implement a single-domain dialogue system by using Rasa.

Here is a simple example for intent classification and NER. A user inputs `I want to eat pizza`. The NLU module can quickly recognize that the user's intent is `Restaurant Search` and the key entity is `pizza`. With intent and key entities, it helps the following DM module to make queries in the backend database to extract target information or continue more rounds of conversation to fill in the other missing slots to complete the question.

From an NLP and ML point of view, intent recognition is a typical text classification task, and slot filling is a typical ER task.

Both tasks need label data. Here is an example of the labels. It consists of intents such as `greet`, `affirm`, `restaurant_search`, and `medical`. Within the intent of `restaurant_search`, it also contains a `food` type of entity. Within the intent of `medical`, it also contains a `disease` type of entity. In reality, we will need way more label data to be able to train a working model.

Here are some training data samples used by the Rasa framework (we will introduce this in the next section). The data format clearly shows that it contains text and labels:

```
{
    "common_examples": [{
        "text": "Hello",
        "intent": "greet",
        "entities": []
    },
```

```
    {
        "text": "Good Morning",
        "intent": "greet",
        "entities": []
    },
    {
        "text": "Where can I find a place for ramen?",
        "intent": "restaurant_search",
        "entities": [{
            "start": 7,
            "end": 8,
            "value": "ramen",
            "entity": "food"
        }]
    },
    {
        "text": "I'm having a fever. What medicine should I
take?",
        "intent": "medical",
        "entities": [{
            "start": 3,
            "end": 4,
            "value": "fever",
            "entity": "disease"
        }]
    }
  ]
}
```

At a first glance, this seems very similar to the rule-based AIML data. In fact, we are using that label data to train a much more complicated ML model. This model will be able to generalize way more scenarios compared to a rule-based system—for example, we give `pizza` and `ramen` as examples of food. When the user inputs `cake` and `salad`, a good NLU system should be able to label them as food entities as well.

The user input text will need to go through NLP preprocessing, such as sentence split, tokenization, POS labeling, and so on. For certain applications, it is also important to do **coreference** resolution to replace the original pronouns with complete names to reduce ambiguation.

Then, we need to do feature engineering and model training. Traditionally, there can be many manually engineered features such as `number_of_tokens`, `symbols_in_between`, and `bag_of_words_in_between`. Then, we perform traditional ML classification algorithms such as linear classification or **support-vector machines** (**SVMs**) to do intent classification, and traditional sequential labeling models such as a **hidden Markov model** (**HMM**) and CRF to do ER. On the other hand, we can also use `word2vec` to do UL on a large corpus to embed hidden features of words into word embeddings and input them into DNN models such as **convolutional neural networks** (**CNNs**) or RNNs to do intent classification and ER.

By training a model, we can achieve higher recall so that the system can cover more different kinds of user input. We can also make use of the rule-based modules we mentioned before to generate new features from those high-precision rules, to help us train a better ML model. The whole architecture is illustrated in the following diagram:

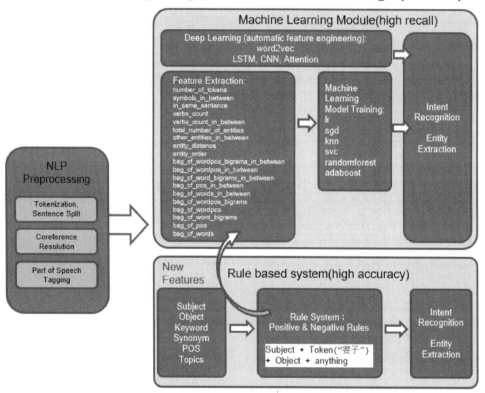

Figure 1.8 – A complex NLU system

Later, we will see how Rasa works in its NLU module to implement NLP in an efficient and open style.

Dialogue Management (DM)

DM decides the current action of a user according to previous conversations. DM is the control center for the process of human-machine conversation and is particularly important for multi-turn task-oriented dialogue systems. The main task of the DM module is to coordinate and manage the whole conversation flow. By analyzing and maintaining the context, the DM module decides if a user's intent is clear enough and information in the entity slots is good enough to start database queries or perform corresponding actions.

When the DM module thinks the information from user input is not complete or too ambiguous, it will start managing a multi-turn conversation context and keep prompting the user to get more information or provide the user with possible items to choose from. DM is responsible for storing and maintaining the current conversation status, the user's action history, the system's action history, and potential results from the knowledge base. When DM decides that it has clearly got all the information needed, it then converts the user's request into a corresponding query into the database (for example, a knowledge graph) to search for the right information or act to complete the task (for example, checking out for shopping, calling a friend's number with Siri, or pulling up a curtain with smart home devices).

The following diagram shows the workflow and functions of DM:

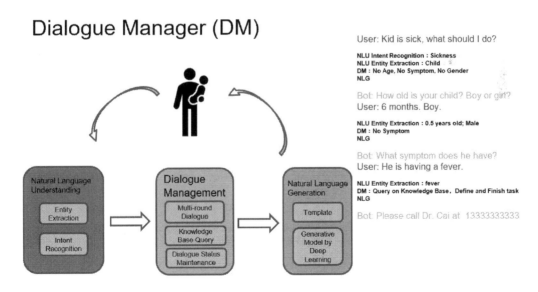

Figure 1.9 – DM in the dialogue system

In real-life use cases, DM is responsible for many small tasks and is highly customized according to product requirements. Many implementations of DM use a rule-based system, and it's not an easy task to either code or maintain it. In recent work, including Rasa, people have started to model the DM status into a sequential labeling SL task. Some advanced work makes use of deep RL, where a user-simulation module is added. We will see later how Rasa implements the DM module in an easy and elegant way with Rasa Core.

Natural Language Generation (NLG)

NLG converts the agent's response into human-readable text. There are mainly two ways of doing this: template-based methods or DL-based methods. The template-based methods create simple responses without too much flexibility. However, as templates are designed by humans, they generally have great readability for humans. DL-based methods can generate flexible and personalized responses. However, as it is automatically generated by DNNs, it is difficult to control the quality and stability of the results. In real situations, people tend to use the template-based method and add new functionalities (for example, choose randomly from a pool of templates) to add more flexibility.

NLG is almost the last challenging mile in human-machine interaction. For a chitchat bot, we normally apply a Seq2Seq generative model to a large volume of corpus and directly generate a response to the user's input. However, this does not normally work for a customer service chatbot that is task-oriented and only for a vertical domain. Users need accurate and concise responses to their inquiries. We are still working toward one day where we have lots of data to train a working model that generates texts that almost come from a real human being—perhaps models such as **GPT3** already achieve this.

Still, most of the current NLG modules use rule-based templates. This is like the reverse operation for slot filling, to fill results into a template and generate a response to users. More advanced works also use DL to automatically generate templates with slots based on training data.

There are also some works that try to use DL to train an **end-to-end** (**E2E**) task-oriented chatbot. Some researchers tried to convert each of the NLU, DM, and NLG modules into DL modules. Some also add a user simulation to train an E2E RL model. Another important piece of academic research work is on memory networks. A memory network is similar to Seq2Seq and encodes the entire knowledge base into a complicated DNN and then combines this with encoded questions to decode to a target answer. This work was applied to machine reading tasks such as the **Stanford Question Answering Dataset** (**SQuAD**) competition from Stanford University and got some great results. As for task-oriented chatbots, this is still pioneering work and needs to be tested.

Text to Speech (TTS)

TTS converts normal language text into speech. TTS has been developed over many years, and there are mature solutions in the industry that are production-ready. In real-life use cases, as with ASR, we tend to use the TTS engine or service provided by professional vendors. We will not cover TTS in this book.

So far, we have learned a lot of necessary knowledge about chatbots. It's now time to do something real. In the next chapter, we will introduce basic knowledge of the Rasa framework, which is a conversational AI framework for real production.

Introduction to the Rasa framework

Rasa is an open source ML framework to construct chatbots and intelligent assistants. Rasa's modular and flexible design enables developers to easily build new extensions and functionalities. Rasa covers almost all the functions needed for building a conversation system and is currently the mainstream open source conversational system framework.

The Rasa framework consists of mainly four parts, outlined as follows:

- **NLU**: Extract user's intent and key context information
- **Core**: Choose the best response and action according to dialogue history
- **Channel and action**: Connect chatbot to users and backend services
- Helper functions such as **Tracker Store**, **Lock Store**, and **Event Broker**

Why Rasa?

There are many options for building chatbots. These solutions can be divided into two types: closed source solutions and open source solutions. Closed source solutions have disadvantages of high cost, vendor lock-in, risk of data leakage, and the inability to implement custom functions. Open source solutions do not have these problems. A disadvantage of open source solutions is that users need to carefully choose a good chatbot framework: this should have large-scale concurrency and powerful functions, be easy to learn, and have an active community. Rasa has all these features: built-in enterprise-grade concurrency capabilities, rich functions covering all the needs of chatbots, rich documents and tutorials, and a huge global community. This is why the Rasa framework ranks first in the number of stars on GitHub among all chatbot frameworks. Many companies have successfully built their own chatbots using Rasa.

Are you curious about how these powerful features of the Rasa framework are implemented? In the next chapter, we will introduce the architecture of Rasa.

System architecture

Rasa contains two main parts—namely, **Rasa** and the **Rasa software development kit** (**Rasa SDK**). Within Rasa, there are also **NLU** and **Core**.

Rasa NLU converts a user's input into intents and entities. This is known as NLU.

Rasa Core decides the next action based on current and history dialogue records (including outputs from Rasa NLU). Such actions can be replying to a particular message from a user or calling some `Action` class that is customized to the user.

Rasa offers Rasa SDK to help developers build their customized actions. Most bots call some kind of external service to accomplish a task—for example, a weather bot will call the API provided by the weather information service to get the current weather information, while a food-booking bot will call external services to make payments and food bookings. In Rasa, this kind of action that depends on business contexts is called a customized action. A customized action runs in an individual server process, so it is also called Action Server. The Action Server communicates with Rasa Core through **HyperText Transfer Protocol** (**HTTP**).

A complete chatbot also needs a friendly UI. Rasa supports many popular **instant messaging** (**IM**) applications and connects to them through Rasa channels.

The core working process for Rasa is represented in the following diagram:

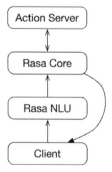

Figure 1.10 – Core working process of Rasa

The software architecture of Rasa is carefully designed to follow the theory of Conway's law—organizations design systems that mirror their communication structure. Rasa NLU and Rasa Core work closely together and are organized into one package called **Rasa**. Rasa SDK is another individual software package. The reason behind this design is that Rasa NLU and Rasa Core are normally developed by the algorithm team, while Customized Actions are developed by the Python engineering team. Those two teams can be decoupled and developed, deployed, and improved independently to improve working efficiency.

Installing Rasa

Before we jump into how to actually install Rasa through the command line, let's talk about **virtual environments** in Python. What is a virtual environment and why do we talk about it? In most cases, Python applications—especially large applications—need to use third-party packages. Since different Python applications may require different versions of the same third-party package, this means that a Python installation cannot meet the requirements of each application. Python's official solution for this is to create a virtual environment for each Python application. A virtual environment is a directory containing a complete Python installation, in which users can install any third-party package without any impact outside the directory. This means that the virtual environment and the system environment and other virtual environments are completely isolated, and they will not affect each other at all.

Although this step is optional in technical but isolating Python projects, using virtual environments has already become the de facto standard in the Python world, so please remember to always create a virtual environment for your Python project. Tools such as the `venv` module of the Python standard library (`https://docs.python.org/3.7/tutorial/venv.html`), **virtualenv** (`https://virtualenv.pypa.io/en/latest/`), and **virtualenvwrapper** (`https://virtualenvwrapper.readthedocs.io/en/latest/`) can help you create a virtual environment easily.

After we create and activate our virtual environment, it is very easy to install Rasa. Simply run the following `pip` command in the command line:

```
pip install rasa
```

The pipeline of a Rasa project

Here are the steps to build a complete Rasa project:

1. Project initialization.
2. Prepare NLU training data.

3. Configure the NLU model.

4. Prepare the story data.

5. Define the domain.

6. Configure the core model.

7. Train the model.

8. Test the chatbot.

9. Let real customers use the chatbot.

We will introduce the NLU part of the pipeline in *Chapter 2, Natural Language Understanding in Rasa*, and the story part in *Chapter 3, Rasa Core*, and the test part in *Chapter 9, Testing and Production Deployment*.

Rasa command line

Some common Rasa commands are shown in the following table:

Command	Function
rasa init	Create a new project that includes sample models, configurations, and actions.
rasa train	Use NLU training data, story data, and configuration files to train a model. By default, the model will be saved in the ./models folder.
rasa interactive	Interactive training: let the user correct possible errors by directing interaction with the bot and export the dialog data.
rasa run	Run the Rasa server.
rasa shell	Same as rasa run, plus open the **command-line interface (CLI)** to interact with the bot.
rasa run actions	Run the Rasa action server.
rasa x	Start the Rasa X server (if Rasa X is not installed, there will be warnings).
rasa -h	Print out helper functions for Rasa commands.

Figure 1.11 – Rasa commands

Creating a sample project

After successful installation of Rasa, the user can start to use Rasa's built-in tools to create a sample project by running the following command:

```
rasa init
```

The Rasa `init` tool will ask about the project path (by default, this is the current path) and whether to train the model immediately after project creation (by default, this is `Yes`, but developers can choose `No` and run `rasa train` later to train models themselves).

After the successful creation of a sample project, the following files are created:

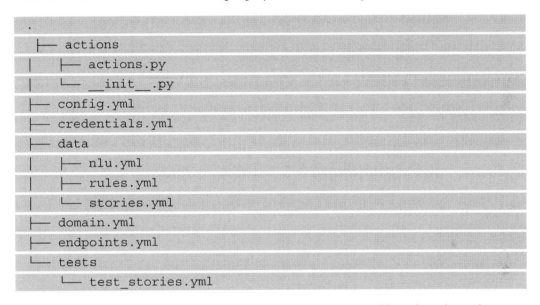

```
.
├── actions
│   ├── actions.py
│   └── __init__.py
├── config.yml
├── credentials.yml
├── data
│   ├── nlu.yml
│   ├── rules.yml
│   └── stories.yml
├── domain.yml
├── endpoints.yml
└── tests
    └── test_stories.yml
```

Congratulations! You have just created your first Rasa project. Although we haven't introduced the Rasa framework in detail, the data and configuration of the sample Rasa project are all ready, so we can start this bot as a playground. After the model training is complete (you can do this when you create a project or use the `rasa train` command for training), we can use the following command in the terminal to start the interactive client of Rasa:

```
rasa shell
```

You can interact with the bot through the keyboard. Here is an example of this:

```
Your input -> Hello
Hey! How are you?
```

```
Your input -> I am fine
Great, carry on!
```

In the following chapters, we will cover all the key files in the sample project and introduce from scratch all the parts and functions of Rasa.

Summary

In this chapter, we have introduced fundamental knowledge of chatbots and the Rasa framework, we have shown how to build a chatbot in theory, and we had a brief introduction to the Rasa framework: its architecture, work pipeline, and CLI.

In the next chapter, we will dive into the NLU part of the Rasa framework.

Further reading

For more information on the topics covered in this chapter, please refer to the following links:

- *Python Machine Learning - Third Edition*: https://www.packtpub.com/product/python-machine-learning-third-edition/9781789955750

- *Python Natural Language Processing Cookbook*: https://www.packtpub.com/product/python-natural-language-processing-cookbook/9781838987312

- Developer portal of Rasa: https://rasa.com/docs/

2
Natural Language Understanding in Rasa

In this chapter, we introduce how to implement **Natural Language Understanding (NLU)** in Rasa.

Rasa NLU is responsible for intent recognition and entity extraction. For example, if the user input is *What's the weather like tomorrow in New York?*, Rasa NLU needs to extract that the intent of the user is *asking for weather*, and the corresponding entity names and type, for example, the date is *tomorrow*, and the location is *New York*.

Rasa NLU uses supervised learning algorithms to fulfill this function. A proper number of examples including intent and entity information are needed for training the NLU model. Rasa NLU has a very flexible software architecture design and supports various kinds of algorithms. The implementations of those algorithms are called components. Components also need to be carefully configured and maintain a correct dependency relationship between their upstream and downstream components. Rasa NLU introduces pipelines as the component configuration system to achieve this.

You can learn Rasa NLU's architecture, configuration methods, and how to train and inference through this chapter. Finally, you will check and deepen your understanding of this knowledge through the practice project.

We will introduce the core elements of Rasa NLU one by one. In particular, we will cover the following topics:

- The format of NLU training data
- Rasa NLU components
- Configuring your Rasa NLU via a pipeline
- The output of Rasa NLU
- Training and serving Rasa NLU
- Practice – building the NLU part of a medical bot

Technical requirements

You can find all the files for this chapter in the `ch02` directory of the GitHub repository at `https://github.com/PacktPublishing/Conversational-AI-with-RASA`.

The format of NLU training data

In the previous chapter, we created an example project by using a command-line tool of Rasa. The project layout is as follows:

```
.
├── actions
│   ├── actions.py
│   └── __init__.py
├── config.yml
├── credentials.yml
├── data
│   ├── nlu.yml
│   ├── rules.yml
│   └── stories.yml
├── domain.yml
├── endpoints.yml
└── tests
    └── test_stories.yml
```

The data/nlu.yml file in the project acts as the training data file for Rasa NLU. The training data file is written in **YAML** (short for **YAML Ain't Markup Language**) format. YAML is a general format for data storage and exchange. It is human-readable and supports a wide range of programming languages.

Before we dive deeper into the specification of training data, here, let me show you a small sample. It will help you grasp the basic concept of what training data is, and make it easier to understand our follow-up explanation. The content of the sample (the data/nlu.yml file) is as follows:

```
version: "2.0"
nlu:
  - intent: intent_name_one
    examples: |
      - This is a sentence that acts as a training example.
      - hello
      - hi
  - intent: intent_name_two
    examples: |
      - This is just another training sample.
      - good night
      - bye
  - intent: intent_name_N
    examples: |
      - yes
      - indeed
      - of course
```

The training data of Rasa NLU is in a list with a key called nlu. In that list, each element is a dictionary, and the functionalities of different dictionaries are defined by specific keys in the dictionary. The specific keys are intent, synonym, regex, and lookup. The intent is mandatory, while the other three keys are optional and thus not in official examples.

Now we will introduce each part in detail. Let's start with the intent field.

The intent field – storing NLU samples

A key of intent indicates that the current object is for storing the training samples. The corresponding value of `intent` is the intent name. Please note that any characters (including Unicode characters) can be used in the intent name, but the / character should not be included, because Rasa has reserved this character and it has a special meaning, which we will introduce later in *Chapter 5, Working with Response Selector to Handle Chitchat and FAQs*. In the training sample object, there is a list named `examples`. Each list contains a training sample.

The following is an example of the training sample:

```
- intent: greet
  examples: |
    - hey
    - hello
    - hi
    - hello there
    - good morning
    - good evening
    - morning
    - hey there
    - let's go
    - hey dude
    - good morning
    - good evening
    - good afternoon
```

The normal character within the training data can be directly written down as the character itself. Entities are written as the Markdown URL expression, namely [entity value] (entity type). Entity value is within [and], followed by entity type within (and).

For example, `What's the weather like [tomorrow](date) in [New York] (city)?`

Here, `tomorrow` (entity value) is `date` (entity type), and `New York` (entity value) is `city` (entity type).

Rasa adds an extra syntax for more complicated labels: [entity value]{"key": "value", ...}. Here, {"key": "value", ...} is a valid JSON dictionary. Under this labeling syntax, [entity value](entity type) is just the simplified version of [entity value]{"entity": "entity type"}. The valid keys also include rule, group, and value. The rule and group keys correspond to labels in entities' roles and groups. The value key is used to label the synonyms of the current entity value.

For example, What's the weather like [tomorrow]{"entity": "date"} in [New York]{"entity": "city", "value": "New York City"}?

In the next section, we will talk about the synonym field.

The synonym field – storing synonyms and aliases

The key for synonym indicates that the object is for storing synonym information. For example, *bike* is a synonym of *bicycle*.

This feature is used during the inference step when the EntitySynonymMapper component is activated (we will cover it later) to replace the synonym of the entity value with its *standard* word.

Here is a complete example of synonym configuration:

```
nlu:
  - synonym: bike
    examples: |
      - bicycle
      - mountain bike
      - road bike
      - folding bike
```

This configuration tells Rasa that if the extracted entity value is bicycle, mountain bike, road bike, or folding bike, it will be replaced by the standard word bike. This feature will only modify the entity value and will not change the entity type.

Note that synonym is used to standardize the entity values *after* entities are recognized by the NLU algorithm. Synonym configuration will not improve the entity extraction, but only help the following component on the actions by standardizing the entity value.

Next, we will introduce the lookup field.

The lookup field – providing extra features by using lookup tables

The `lookup` key indicates that the object is for storing lookup tables. If users can be provided with extra features, the performance of components for intent recognition and entity extraction can be improved. One of the ways to provide extra features is to give a keyword dictionary. This keyword dictionary is the lookup table.

Here is an example of `lookup` (a small cities list):

```
nlu:
  - lookup: city
    examples: |
      - New York
      - Chicago
      - San Francisco
      - Huston
```

When the data in this keyword dictionary matches the text, the lookup table will set the key value to be `1` in the corresponding position and `0` on the unmatched positions, as follows:

Figure 2.1 – An example of how a lookup table works

As shown in *Figure 2.1*, if there are `New York` and `San Francisco` in the list of cities, the sentence **Book a flight from New York to San Francisco** will have the table lookup feature `[0 0 0 0 1 1 0 1 1]`. Legal city names can be exhaustively listed, so they can be made into a lookup table. With the support of lookup table features, the model has more knowledge to make predictions. The model will focus on the words and sentences marked by these lookup features. Therefore, even if there are city names that do not appear in the training data during inference, the model still has the ability to correctly extract the city names with the help of the lookup features.

In the next section, we talk about the regex field, which has a similar function.

The regex field – providing extra features by using regular expressions

The `regex` key indicates that the object is for storing regular expressions. Regular expressions are used to match certain patterns and generate pattern match results as a new feature for the entity extraction or intent recognition components to improve performance.

In Rasa, regular expressions use Python regular expressions as the backend engine. You can use it in the training data file as follows:

```
nlu:
  - regex: help
    examples: |
      - \bhelp\b
```

There are many advantages of using regular expressions. For example, if we use a normal entity extraction component to look for entities such as *personal security numbers*, *telephone numbers*, and *IP addresses*, it is difficult to get good accuracy. However, by using regular expressions, we can easily design the patterns to match those entity formats. The regular expression is especially efficient and powerful when there are certain patterns in the target entities.

Now let's see how regular expressions work in Rasa:

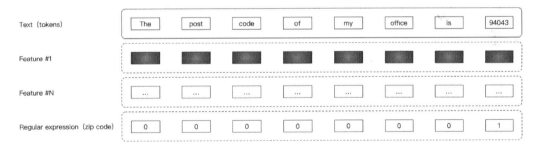

Figure 2.2 – An example of how regular expressions work

The text in *Figure 2.2* contains a zip code. In the case of using the default features, it is difficult for the Named Entity Recognition (NER) component to correctly extract the zip code. For people, it is an easy task because there is an obvious pattern: five digits. The regular expression can be expressed as `\d{5}`, and the token feature that matches the zip code is `1`. Otherwise, it is `0`.

Now that we have learned how to use `lookup` and `regex`, in the next section, we will summarize the usage of these two features.

Using regex and lookup

There are normally two ways of using `regex` and `lookup` in Rasa:

- As part of the features for the entity extraction component:

  A good entity extraction component should be able to make use of the information we provide to it and discover patterns from the features. Note that the features we provide are only to recommend to the model that, for example, there may be a telephone number here, but we are not certain. This is possible because there may be a coincidence that the same number we think is a telephone number may also appear in someone's personal security number. The model needs to check the context to decide whether it should take our recommendation or not. A regular expression is only to help models get more supporting features. Developers still need to generate the training samples for intents and entities.

  In order to have the model be able to learn the correlation between lookup table features and target predictions, developers should make sure that in the training data, there are patterns that come from the lookup table. If there are no patterns at all from the lookup table, the model will not be able to find the correlation between the prediction target and regex or lookup table. Developers also should make sure that there is no error or noise in the lookup table data. Otherwise, if model relies heavily on regex or lookup table features, the performance will decrease.

- As an entity extraction component:

  The `RegexEntityExtractor` component in Rasa can extract entities with `regex` and `lookup` data. This is totally rule-based but can be efficient in certain use cases.

Now that we have learned how to define the training data, in the next section, we will introduce components that consume that training data.

Overview of Rasa NLU components

Rasa NLU is a pipeline-based general framework. This gives Rasa great flexibility.

A pipeline defines the data processing order for each component. There are dependencies between certain components. One failure in such dependency requirements will fail the whole pipeline. Rasa NLU checks the dependency requirements for each and every component. If any of those dependency requirements fail, Rasa will stop the program and give corresponding errors and warnings.

One NLU application normally includes both an intent recognition task and entity extraction task. To accomplish those tasks, here is a typical Rasa NLU pipeline:

Figure 2.3 – A typical Rasa NLU pipeline

Let's look at the components within this typical Rasa NLU pipeline:

- **Language model component**: This loads the language model files to support the following components. For example, spaCy and MITIE can be initiated here.

- **Tokenizer component**: This splits text into tokens.

- **Featurizer component**: This extracts features from token sequences. There can be multiple feature extraction components to generate different features.

- **Entity extractor component**: This performs **named entity extraction** on the text using the features provided by the previous components.

- **Intent classifier component**: This classifies text into different user intents according to context. It is also called intent recognition.

- **Structure output**: This organizes the prediction results into structured data and outputs it. This part is not a component but a built-in function within the pipeline. Developers are not able to directly access it as a component.

Rasa NLU's pipeline has the following features:

- The sequential order of components is critical. For example, normally, the entity extraction component cannot work properly unless it has the correct inputs of tokenization results from the previous component. If this is the case, there must be a tokenizer component before the entity extraction component.

- A component is replaceable and can be plugged in with different versions or implementations. For example, you can plug in a tokenizer from **Stanford CoreNLP** or from **spaCy**, and they should both give you reasonable tokenization results.

- Some components are exclusive. For example, you should not have tokenization results from both Stanford CoreNLP and spaCy. Otherwise, there will be confusion.

- Some components can be used simultaneously. For example, you can have both rule-based components and word-embedding-based components for text feature extraction. The features from both components can be used together in the model.

Since typical Rasa pipelines always start with language model components, let's take a closer look at the language model components first.

Language model components

The language model component loads the pre-trained word embedding. When you choose which component, we recommend that you use HFTransformersNLP first (in the newer version of Rasa, use LanguageModelFeaturizer that will be introduced later). This is because HFTransformersNLP usually has better accuracy. If you cannot use HFTransformersNLP due to limitations in computing power, memory, or disk capacity, then it is recommended that you choose from SpacyNLP and MitieNLP based on the tests on your dataset.

Here are all language model components currently supported by Rasa:

Components	Model	Notes
SpacyNLP	spaCy	Pre-trained spaCy models need to be downloaded in advance. For more details, please check the spaCy official website.
MitieNLP	MITIE	MITIE needs a pre-trained model. You need to pre-train or download a model from the internet.
HFTransformersNLP	Transformer	To use the HFTransformersNLP component, install Rasa Open Source with pip install rasa[transformers]. HFTransformersNLP is deprecated in the newer version of Rasa 2.x, and LanguageModelFeaturizer now implements its behavior.

Figure 2.4 – Built-in language model components

In the next section, we will introduce tokenizer components.

Tokenizer components

Tokenizer components are closely related to languages. No tokenizer can support all languages. You should choose the appropriate tokenizer according to your target language. WhitespaceTokenizer can be used for space-splittable languages. That means if your target language is English, you should use WhitespaceTokenizer. For the Chinese language, you should use JiebaTokenizer. MitieTokenizer (which uses a pre-trained model from MitieNLP) is usually used for word segmentation in languages (such as Japanese, Chinese, or Korean) that do not use space to split words. Your chosen tokenizer should support the language used by your pre-trained model. SpacyTokenizer currently supports about 63 languages. You can check whether your target language is on the list or not at https://spacy.io/usage/models#languages.

There are the tokenizer components Rasa supports:

Components	Requirement	Model	Notes
WhitespaceTokenizer			Tokenizer using whitespaces as a separator
JiebaTokenizer	Jieba	Conditional Random Field	For Chinese
MitieTokenizer	MITIE	Structured SVM	
SpacyTokenizer	spaCy	Multiple models	

Figure 2.5 – Built-in tokenizer components

It is also not difficult to extend Rasa to support other tokenizers thanks to Rasa NLU's pipeline design. All we need is to implement a tokenization component ourselves and we will show you how in *Chapter 8, Working Principles and Customization of Rasa.*

Now we already have components that can tokenize text to tokens. In the next section, we will introduce featurizer components that can transform text into features.

Featurizer components

For both entity extraction and intent classification, features provided from upstream components are required. Developers can use multiple components to do feature extraction. Those components have implemented feature union operation so developers can freely choose and combine feature extraction components.

Generally, we recommend using LanguageModelFeaturizer, because it supports many languages and has outstanding performance. If you cannot use LanguageModelFeaturizer, then we recommend you to try ConveRTFeaturizer and SpacyFeaturizer. If none of the above featurizers supports your target language, then you can try using MitieFeaturizer and your own pre-trained model. If the Rasa model does not work well, then you can consider adding LexicalSyntacticFeaturizer, which will add additional features to the input. Using RegexFeaturizer can provide features based on dictionary and regular expressions for subsequent intent classification and NER components.

All the featurizers are shown in the following table:

Component	Requirements	Notes
MitieFeaturizer	MitieNLP	
SpacyFeaturizer	SpacyNLP	
ConveRTFeaturizer	Tokenization	Based on ConveRT from Poly AI.
LanguageModelFeaturizer	Tokenization	Based on Transformers from HuggingFace.
RegexFeaturizer	Tokenization	This component reads regular expression configurations from training data.
CountVectorsFeaturizer	Tokenization	Based on Bag-of-words model. Usually used in toy projects.
LexicalSyntacticFeaturizer	Tokenization	Gives linguistic features, for example, whether it is the head or tail of a sentence or whether it is a number.

Figure 2.6 – Built-in featurizer components

In the next section, we will introduce entity extraction components that can extract named entities from the text features.

Entity extraction components

Rasa supports multiple entity extraction components. Most of those components should not be used together, with a few exceptions that can be used together under certain conditions. Some components can only produce predefined entities and cannot be trained on developers' own entities.

We recommend that you try DIETClassifier first, because it usually has better performance. If the extracted entities you want include time, date, URL, phone number, and email, then you can consider using DucklingEntityExtractor. It can help you extract these entities and convert them into structured data without training. You can visit https://github.com/facebook/duckling for a list of all the entities it supports. If you want to extract entities such as people's names, place names, and organization names, then you can try SpacyEntityExtractor. It can help you automatically extract without training. You can see the list of entities supported by each language model at https://spacy.io/models. If your entities are a small finite set or can be matched by regular expressions, then you will find RegexEntityExtractor very useful.

Here, we list all entity extraction components and give some brief descriptions as follows:

Components	Requirement	Model	Notes
CRFEntityExtractor	sklearn-srfsuite	**Conditional Random Field (CRF)**	
SpacyEntityExtractor	spaCy	Averaged perceptron	Pretrained entities.
MitieEntityExtractor	MITIE	Structured SVM	
EntitySynonymMapper	Existing entities		Standardization of synonyms.
DIETClassifier	Tensorflow	CRF on top of a transformer	
RegexEntityExtractor			Use lookups and regular expressions in the training data.
DucklingEntityExtractor			We need to run a Duckling server for it.

Figure 2.7 – Built-in entity extraction components

For now, we already know the components that can extract named entities for us. In the next section, we will introduce components that do the job of intent classification.

Intent classifier components

We recommend trying DIETClassifier first, which is the best choice in most cases. If you cannot use DIETClassifier, then you can choose from MitieIntentClassifier and SklearnIntentClassifier based on the tests on your dataset. FallbackClassifier is a special component for handling fallback situations, and we will discuss it in *Chapter 4, Handling Business Logic*.

Here we list all the intent classifier (also called intent recognition) built-in components in Rasa:

Components	Requirement	Model	Notes
MitieIntentClassifier	MITIE	Structured SWM	
SklearnIntentClassifier	Scikit-learn		
KeywordIntentClassifier			Based on the keywords matching. Usually used in toy projects.
DIETClassifier	TensorFlow	CRF on top of a transformer	
FallbackClassifier			Set intent value to nlu_ fallback if the other component gives too low a confidence score on intent.

Figure 2.8 – Built-in intent classifier components

Note that Rasa develops its own **Dual Intent Entity Transformer** (**DIET**) technology in `DIETClassifier` that supports multi-task modeling for both entity extraction and intent recognition.

So far, we have introduced all the components of NLU processing. In Rasa, there is a special component that can help us easily deal with FAQ-like conversations. In the next section, we will introduce it.

Handling frequently asked questions by using a response selector

For simple question-answering problems such as **Frequently Asked Questions** (**FAQs**), NLU alone can easily tackle the tasks. Rasa implements the `ResponseSelector` component to achieve this.

So far, we have learned the different types of components. In the next section, we will discuss how the Rasa framework configures and orchestrates components.

Configuring your Rasa NLU via a pipeline

As mentioned in the previous section, Rasa NLU is a general framework based on pipelines. This gives Rasa NLU maximum flexibility.

What is a pipeline?

A pipeline in Rasa defines the dependency relationship and data flow direction between the different components, and it allows the developer to configure each of the components. The pipeline gives the Rasa framework great flexibility and extensibility. We will discuss the extensibility advantages of pipelines in *Chapter 8, Working Principles and Customization of Rasa*.

In the next section, we will learn how to use the pipeline to orchestrate components.

Configuring a pipeline

The configuration format Rasa NLU uses is YAML. Here is an example of a configuration file of Rasa NLU:

```
language: en
pipeline:
   - name: WhitespaceTokenizer
   - name: RegexFeaturizer
```

```yaml
  - name: LexicalSyntacticFeaturizer
  - name: CountVectorsFeaturizer
  - name: CountVectorsFeaturizer
    analyzer: char_wb
    min_ngram: 1
    max_ngram: 4
  - name: DIETClassifier
    epochs: 100
  - name: EntitySynonymMapper
  - name: ResponseSelector
    epochs: 100
  - name: FallbackClassifier
    threshold: 0.3
    ambiguity_threshold: 0.1
policies:
  # It has nothing to do with NLU, so it is omitted here
```

There are generally two main keys in the configuration file of Rasa NLU: `language` and `pipeline`. In `config.yml`, there is also a `policies` key, but it is used to configure dialogue management. We will discuss dialogue management and this key in *Chapter 3, Rasa Core*.

Language defines which language Rasa NLU is going to process. Rasa itself is a language-agnostic chatbot framework and can support multiple languages. However, the components to be used are likely to be dependent on the language choice. Some components can only support specific languages. For example, a tokenizer may only support one or two languages and will not be able to support all the languages. The `jieba` tokenizer that is widely used for Chinese language processing cannot handle Japanese tokenization. Also, some components contain different model packages for different languages. spaCy supports different model packages specifically in different languages.

The language configuration in Rasa gives the target language information to components. If the language is not supported, the component can throw exceptions to developers to suggest switching to another valid component. If the component supports multiple language model packages, the language configuration can also guide the component to load the corresponding model package. For example, in spaCy, the model package with the same name as the language configuration will be loaded by default.

The configuration format is `language: <lang_code>`, where `<lang_code>` is the language code under the ISO 639-1 standard. The code for English is `en`, and the code for Chinese is `zh`. If Rasa cannot find this configuration, it will set it to be `en` by default.

The pipeline is the core of the configuration file. It consists of a list (in YAML, it starts with `-`). Each element in the list is a dictionary (in YAML, it is in the format of `name:xxx`). Each dictionary corresponds to a pipeline component. Each component is defined by the name key in the dictionary. The other keys are configurations to its component and are customized by each component. Rasa is responsible for transmitting the component configuration information to the corresponding component during initialization.

In the previous example, there are six components. Note that `CountVectorsFeaturizer` appears twice in the pipeline, which is allowed by Rasa. And in the second time, it contains three configuration items: `analyzer:"char_wb"`, `min_ngram:1`, and `max_ngram:4`.

How to choose the components in the pipeline is a difficult problem. This is related to your target language, deployment environment, application scenarios, and desired features. Different target languages may require different components (for example, different tokenizers or different language model components). Different deployment environments may make certain components unusable (for example, when deployed on low-resource computers, some components will not be suitable). Different application scenarios may require the use of different components to achieve the best results (for example, in some scenarios, using `RegexEntityExtractor` is better than `DIETClassifier`). The function of the dialogue robot will also lead to different component selection (whether to support chitchat or FAQs will determine whether to use the `ResponseSelector` component).

Here, we recommend a basic NLU configuration suitable for English as the target language. On this basis, you can add other components (described in later chapters) according to functional requirements. The basic NLU configuration is as follows:

```
language: en
pipeline:
  - name: WhitespaceTokenizer
  - name: LanguageModelFeaturizer
    model_name: "bert"
    model_weights: "rasa/LaBSE"
  - name: RegexFeaturizer
  - name: DIETClassifier
```

In our experience, this configuration of `LanguageModelFeaturizer` + `DIETClassifier` has good performance. It can be adapted to many target languages with slight changes (such as the tokenizer and the `model_weights` parameter of `LanguageModelFeaturizer`). `RegexFeaturizer` can make good use of the dictionary and regular expression features and is suitable for many application scenarios.

Now we have learned how to configure Rasa NLU. In the next section, we will talk about the output of Rasa NLU.

The output of Rasa NLU

In order to properly debug Rasa NLU, developers should understand its output format.

The output format of Rasa NLU's inference is as follows:

```
{
    "text": "show me chinese restaurants",
    "intent": "restaurant_search",
    "entities": [
        {
            "start": 8,
            "end": 15,
            "value": "chinese",
            "entity": "cuisine",
            "extractor": "CRFEntityExtractor",
            "confidence": 0.854,
            "processors": []
        }
    ]
}
```

It contains three main parts: `text`, `intent`, and `entities`. The `text` field is the raw text the user inputs. It is just a string and does not have a complex structure, so we will not set up a subsection for it. The `intent` and `entities` fields are complex structures; we will discuss them in the following subsections.

Let's start with the introduction of the `intent` field.

The intent field – the purpose of the user's utterance

The `intent` field can be a string representing the intent:

```
"intent": "restaurant_search"
```

The `intent` field can also be a dictionary containing the intent and its confidence from the intent classifier:

```
"intent": {
  "name": "greet",
  "confidence": 0.9968444108963013
}
```

The `intent` field may also give the `intent_ranking` showing the confidence of other possible intents:

```
{
  "intent": {
    "name": "greet",
    "confidence": 0.9968444108963013
  },
  "entities": [],
  "intent_ranking": [
    {
      "name": "greet",
      "confidence": 0.9968444108963013
    },
<!-- similar outputs are omitted -->
    {
      "name": "mood_great",
      "confidence": 5.138086999068037e-05
    }
  ],
  "text": "hello"
}
```

In the next section, we will cover the `entities` field.

The entities field – key parameters of user's utterance

The results of entity extraction are represented by the start and end position of the entity within the text, the entity value (`value` field), and entity type (`entity` field). Besides, there can be other supporting information, for example, the `confidence` and `extractor` fields. Note that the entity position may be inconsistent with the raw text, because some components may perform certain processing steps on the raw data to facilitate developers. For example, date information can be standardized by the component.

Here is an example of `entities`:

```
"entities": [
    {
        "start": 8,
        "end": 15,
        "value": "chinese",
        "entity": "cuisine",
        "extractor": "CRFEntityExtractor",
        "confidence": 0.854,
        "processors": []
    },
    <!-- other entities -->
]
```

It is worth noting that the location of entities in the text uses Python indexing and slicing conventions. This means that the position starts at 0. The start position is included, and the end position is not included. In the example, starting position 8 is the starting position of the entity value, but position 14 (not 15) is the position of the last entity value.

So far, we have learned the `intent` and `entities` fields. In the next section, we will introduce other possible fields that Rasa may output.

Other possible fields

There are also other fields that may be output by components. For example:

```
{
    "text": "show me chinese restaurants",
    "intent": "restaurant_search",
    "entities": [
```

```
{
    "start": 8,
    "end": 15,
    "value": "chinese",
    "entity": "cuisine",
    "extractor": "CRFEntityExtractor",
    "confidence": 0.854,
    "processors": []
}
],
"response_selector": {
  "default": {
    "response": {
      "name": null,
      "confidence": 0.0
    },
    "ranking": []
  }
}
}
```

From the example, we can see that it has an additional field called `response_selector`; it is generated by the `ResponseSelector` component, which will be introduced in *Chapter 5, Working with Response Selector to Handle Chitchat and FAQs.*

Besides the `ReponseSelector`, there also exist components that generate additional fields. The generated information is useful, such as getting better accuracy or output debug info. Here is a sample additional field from the `DucklingHTTPExtractor` component; its output can help users to get several types of entities without training data:

```
{
  "additional_info":{
    "grain":"day",
    "type":"value",
    "value":"2018-06-21T00:00:00.000-07:00",
    "values":[
      {
```

```
            "grain":"day",
            "type":"value",
            "value":"2018-06-21T00:00:00.000-07:00"
        }
    ]
},
"confidence":1.0,
"end":5,
"entity":"time",
"extractor":"DucklingHTTPExtractor",
"start":0,
"text":"today",
"value":"2018-06-21T00:00:00.000-07:00"
}
```

With the training data and pipeline in place, in the next section, we will start to train and serve Rasa NLU.

Training and running Rasa NLU

Rasa is a very *cohesive* framework. We can use the built-in command-line tools of Rasa that we already introduced in the first chapter to perform tasks such as model training and prediction.

Let's start with model training.

Training our models

We can start training models after we have configured the pipeline and got the training data. Rasa provides developers with commands that can help us train a model quickly. As long as we are using the official project structure, Rasa's commands are able to locate the configuration and data files.

The command for training a model is as follows:

```
rasa train nlu
```

This command will look for training data in the data path, use config.yml as the pipeline configuration, and save the model (a zipped file) into the models path with nlu- as the prefix of the model's name. The length of training time depends on the components used and the size of the training dataset. The log will be printed continuously during the training process, and the user can see the current training progress from it.

After the training command is finished, we can test our model via the command line.

Testing models from the command line

Rasa provides the command to test the model directly from the command line and interact with the model. This command is rasa shell; we already introduced this Rasa command in *Chapter 1, Introduction to Chatbots and the Rasa Framework*. It will run the Rasa server in the background and provide a command-line-based interactive UI to allow users to interact with the Rasa server. You can start using the Rasa shell by typing the following command:

```
rasa shell nlu
```

This command opens the Rasa shell. Developers can do text-based interaction with the model in the shell directly. If there are multiple models (multiple model files under the models path), Rasa will load the most recent model.

To run the Rasa shell with a specific model, run the following command:

```
rasa shell -m models/nlu-<timestamp>.tar.gz
```

Here is the user interface for the Rasa shell:

```
NLU model loaded. Type a message and press enter to parse it.
 Next message:
 hello  <-- This is the user input -->
 {
   "intent": {
     "name": "greet",
      "confidence": 0.9968444108963013
   },
   "entities": [],
   "intent_ranking": [
      {
        "name": "greet",
```

```
      "confidence": 0.9968444108963013
    },
    <-- Some similar outputs are omitted -->
    {
      "name": "mood_great",
      "confidence": 5.138086999068037e-05
    }
  ],
  "response_selector": {
    "default": {
      "response": {
        "name": null,
        "confidence": 0.0
      },
      "ranking": []
    }
  },
  "text": "hello"
}
Next message:
  | <-- Waiting for user's input here -->
```

In the next section, we will introduce how to start a server for inference from other computers.

Starting the Rasa NLU service

The service of Rasa NLU uses a RESTful HTTP API. Start the service by running the following:

```
rasa run --enable-api
```

Now you can send a request to the /model/parse path to use the Rasa NLU prediction service. For example, if we use curl as a client:

```
curl localhost:5005/model/parse -d '{"text":"hello"}'
```

In a real debugging situation, developers can consider using tools such as Postman to send requests and test. In *Figure 2.9*, we show is an example of using Postman to send requests and get results:

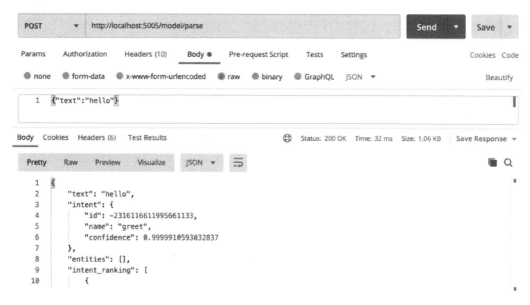

Figure 2.9 – An example of using Postman to send NLU requests and check results

So far, we have learned how to use Rasa NLU in theory. In the next section, we will do some exercises to make sure you understand them correctly.

Practice – building the NLU part of a medical bot

The best way to learn Rasa NLU is by practice. Here, we work on a project to build a simple NLU component for a medical domain chatbot. All the project files can be found under the directory named ch02 in the GitHub repository at `https://github.com/PacktPublishing/Conversational-AI-with-RASA`.

What are the features of our bot?

Our bot supports the following functions:

- Recognize the intent in a medicine inquiry or hospital and department inquiry.
- Extract entities for diseases and symptoms.
- Simple greetings.

How can we implement our bot in Rasa?

Let's follow the official Rasa project structure:

```
.
├── config.yml
├── credentials.yml
├── data
│   └── nlu.yml
├── domain.yml
├── endpoints.yml
└── models
```

In this simple NLU project, there are two files – `credentials.yml` and `endpoints.yml` – that we have not covered yet. We will introduce them in the next chapter. For now, just ignore them. We introduce the other files here. Let's start with the training data.

Creating NLU training data

Generally, NLU training data is stored in the `data/nlu.yml` file. For this project, we have the training data in the following list (the full content of this file has already been provided to you in the GitHub repository):

```
version: "2.0"
nlu:
  - intent: greet
    examples: |
      - Hello
      - Hi
  - intent: goodbye
    examples: |
      - ByeBye
      - bye
  - intent: medicine
    examples: |
      - What medicine should I take if I have a [cold](disease)
      - I am [constipated](disease), what medicine should I
take?
```

```
    - intent: medical_department
      examples: |
        - Which department should I go to when I have a [cold]
(disease)?
        - I have [constipation](disease), which department should
I go to?
    - intent: medical_hospital
      examples: |
        - Which hospital should I go to for my [stomachache]
(disease)?
        - Are there any good hospitals or health centers to
recommend for [weight loss](disease)?
```

In the next section, we will talk about the domain configuration.

Configuring the domain

Generally, Rasa's domain settings are stored in the domain.yml file. For this project, we only need to list all the intents, as follows:

```
version: "2.0"
intents:
  - greet
  - goodbye
  - medicine
  - medical_department
  - medical_hospital
```

Configuring the pipeline

Generally, Rasa's pipeline configuration is stored in the configure.yml file. Since we have only learned the NLU part, we only set up the NLU pipeline configuration:

```
language: en
pipeline:
  - name: WhitespaceTokenizer
  - name: RegexFeaturizer
  - name: LexicalSyntacticFeaturizer
  - name: CountVectorsFeaturizer
  - name: CountVectorsFeaturizer
```

```
    analyzer: char_wb
    min_ngram: 1
    max_ngram: 4
 - name: DIETClassifier
    epochs: 100
policies:
```

In the preceding configuration (the last line), there is a key named `policies` with an empty value. This key is used to configure dialogue management, but we have not learned the dialogue management of Rasa yet (this will be taught in the next chapter). Therefore, the value here is empty.

So far, we have the training data and pipeline. In the next step, we will train the model.

Training NLU models

Run the following command at the project root path to train an NLU model:

```
rasa train nlu
```

After training is done, there will be a model automatically saved as a zipped file in the `models` folder.

In the next step, let's run the model and make some inferences.

Setting up the model server and making inferences

Now we can use the built-in Rasa shell client to test our NLU model. Run the following command at the project root path:

```
rasa shell nlu
```

It gives a command-line user interface like the following:

```
NLU model loaded. Type a message and press enter to parse it.
Next message: <-- The cursor is blinking here. -->
```

Now we can input the testing sentences such as `What medicine should I take if I catch a cold`, and we can get NLU results as follows:

```
{
    "text": "What medicine should I take if I catch a cold",
    "intent": {
```

```
    "id": 179298967045811726,
  "name": "medicine",
  "confidence": 0.9999912977218628
},
"entities": [
  {
    "entity": "disease",
    "start": 41,
    "end": 45,
    "confidence_entity": 0.9994207620620728,
    "value": "cold",
    "extractor": "DIETClassifier"
  }
],
}
```

We see that Rasa returns the results of the intent classification and a list of named entities. In fact, Rasa also returns an intent ranking, as shown in the following code block (this field is only provided by some components):

```
"intent_ranking": [
  {
    "id": 179298967045811726,
    "name": "medicine",
    "confidence": 0.9999912977218628
  },
<-- For brevity, we have omitted some similar items here. -->
  {
    "id": -5857627908142243930,
    "name": "goodbye",
    "confidence": 1.1760136686689293e-07
  }
]
```

Summary

In this chapter, we discussed the NLU part of Rasa. We gave a detailed explanation of the NLU training data structure. We discussed the high-level architecture of pipelines and components. We stepped through an example NLU component of a medical bot. This is an important part of Rasa. At this point, as a reader, you should have understood the architecture of Rasa NLU and how to configure it. You should be able to perform model training and inference operations.

In the next chapter, we will introduce Rasa Core.

3
Rasa Core

In this chapter, we introduce how to implement dialogue management in Rasa. Rasa Core is the component in Rasa that handles dialogue management. Dialogue management is responsible for keeping a record of the conversation context and choosing the next actions accordingly.

The dialogue management system can be divided into four parts. **Dialogue state tracking** updates the dialogue state according to the previous round of dialogue and the previous round of system actions, as well as the user's intentions and entities in the current round. The **dialogue policy** is responsible for outputting dialogue actions according to the dialogue state. The **dialogue action** is based on the decision of the dialogue strategy to interact with the backend interface to complete the actual task execution. And finally, the **dialogue result output** outputs the result of the system operation in a user-friendly way.

In Rasa Core, these functions have all been integrated, and users can use Rasa's dialogue management functions in an end-to-end machine learning-based manner. After reading this chapter, you should be able to understand the components of Rasa's dialogue management system, including **domain**, **story**, **action**, **slot**, and **policy**. You should be able to define your own custom actions and understand how Rasa communicates with instant messaging software. And finally, you should be able to develop simple chatbots.

In particular, we will be covering the following topics:

- Understanding the universe of your bot (domain)
- Training data for dialogue management (stories)
- Reacting to user input (action)
- Understanding the memory of your bot (slots)
- Understanding the decision-maker of your bot (policies)
- Building custom actions using Rasa SDK
- Using channels to communicate with instant messaging software
- Building a tell-the-time bot

Technical requirements

In this chapter, we will introduce a new Python package called `rasa-sdk`. It has exactly the same dependencies as `rasa`. We already introduced this in *Chapter 1, Introduction to Chatbots and the Rasa Framework*. Specifically, you need a Python 3.6, 3.7, or 3.8 environment to successfully install the software.

You can find all the files for this chapter in the `ch03` directory of the GitHub repository at the following URL: `https://github.com/PacktPublishing/Conversational-AI-with-RASA`.

Understanding the universe of your bot (domain)

A domain defines all the information a chatbot needs to know, including `intents`, `entities`, `slots`, `actions`, `forms`, and `responses`. All this information gives clear definitions of the inputs and outputs of a model.

A sample domain file is as follows:

```
intents:
  - greet
  - goodbye
  - affirm
  - thank_you
entities:
```

```
    - name
slots:
  name:
    type: text
responses:
  utter_greet:
    - "hey there {name}!" # {name} is template variable
  utter_goodbye:
    - "goodbye"
    - "bye bye"
  utter_default:
    - "default message"
actions:
  - utter_default
  - utter_greet
  - utter_goodbye
```

In this sample domain file, we can see some fields: `intents`, `entities`, `slots`, `responses`, and `actions`. Since `form` functions are particularly important to the user and they are much more complex than other functions, we will introduce the `form` function in the next chapter; in this chapter, let's simply ignore it.

Let's start with `intents` and `entities`.

Intents and entities

These two fields provide the chatbot with the potential **intents** and **entities** that it needs to handle. We have already given a detailed explanation of what `intents` and `entities` are in *Chapter 2, Natural Language Understanding in Rasa*. In simple terms, the intent is what the bot is trying to accomplish, and the entity represents the key information provided by the user. For example, in the sentence, *how is the weather tomorrow?*, the user's intention (that is, the purpose) is to query the weather, and the query date is tomorrow. The date query is the entity. They should be consistent throughout in Rasa **Natural Language Understanding (NLU)**.

In the next section, we will talk about `slots`.

Slots

The slot defines the information that the chatbot needs to track or memorize during the conversation.

The following is an example showing `slots`:

```
slots:
  priority:
    type: categorical
    values:
      - low
      - medium
      - high
```

In this example, the name of the slot is `priority`. Each slot has a type. Here, the type of slot is `categorical`. Each type owns its specific feature configurations that define the scope of slot values, so that the model can easily convert the slot values into machine learning features (we will cover this later in *Chapter 8, Working Principles and Customization of Rasa*). In this example, the values of the slot are restricted to `low`, `medium`, and `high`. Rasa also allows developers to customize their own slots.

In the following section, we will introduce `actions`.

All possible actions the bot can take (actions)

The action is the output of the dialogue management module. Actions define the things that the chatbot can perform. Some examples are providing users with buttons to click, sending messages to the user, calling an external **Application Programming Interface** (**API**) or querying an internal database, and so on.

In Rasa, actions starting with `utter_` are considered as the user templates. Next, we will talk about the **Natural Language Generation** (**NLG**) part of Rasa: `responses`.

All the predefined replies to users (responses)

Responses define the templates of a chatbot's replies. For example, see the following:

```
responses:
  utter_greet:
    - "Hello {name}!" # {name} is a template variable
  utter_goodbye:
```

```
        - "Goodbye"
        - "Bye" # One of them is randomly chosen if there are
    multiple templates
      utter_default:
        - "This is a default message"
```

There are three templates here: `utter_greet`, `utter_goodbye`, and `utter_default`. All the names of the responses start with `utter_`.

The template string of Rasa supports variables and randomly chooses one of the variations. The `{name}` variable in `utter_greet` here is a variable or a placeholder and will be replaced by the real value of the `name` slot when it is rendered.

Another method is to use `dispatcher.utter_message(template="utter_greet", name="Silly")` to set the real value `Silly` to the template variable `{name}` when we customize the template rendering. There are two template variations, `"Goodbye"` and `"Bye"`, for `utter_goodbye`, and one of them will be randomly chosen when rendered.

Not only simple text responses are supported but also rich responses. Rich responses are similar to common rich text. They are able to hold information other than text, for example, images and buttons. Rich responses in Rasa need support from channels (chat or messenger platforms such as Facebook Messenger or Telegram). For example, refer to the following:

```
responses:
  utter_cheer_up:
    - text: "Here is the picture of the item:"
      image: https://some.url/to/some/image.jpg
```

Another type of rich response is the button, and it needs channel support as well. The following is an example:

```
responses:
  utter_greet:
    - text: "What is your gender?"
      buttons:
        - title: "Male"
          payload: '/set_gender{"gender": "male"}'
        - title: "Female"
          payload: '/set_gender{"gender": "female"}'
```

Here, the `title` field will be displayed to users. When the user clicks on the button, the corresponding `payload` field will be transferred to Rasa.

Developers can define different outputs for different channels. If there are multiple template variations for one response, we can use the `channel` field to assign a specific template variable to a specific channel. For example, refer to the following:

```
responses:
  utter_welcome:
    - text: "Hello, dear Slack users!"
      channel: "slack"
    - text: "Hello, dear users!"
```

Here there are two template variations for `utter_welcome`. The first one with `Hello, dear Slack users!` is bundled to a Slack channel by a defining channel: `slack`. When the response is rendered, if the system detects the user is from the Slack channel, it will use this specific template variation. For more complex outputs, Rasa also supports `custom` fields for developers to customize complex response content.

In some cases, it is not the best choice to retrain the bot just because of changes in the responses, because retraining the model may take a long time and a lot of computing resources. In addition, for complex scenarios, Rasa's built-in template-based response generation is not powerful enough to complete complex response generation. Fortunately, Rasa allows you to delegate the response generation function to an external service. This is called an NLG service. After the external NLG service is enabled, the bot no longer directly renders the template through responses, but instead sends the template rendering request to the NLG service (external HTTP server), and the service returns the generated response. Since this feature is rarely used, we will not continue to talk about it in depth. You can learn more by reading the official documentation, available at the following URL: `https://rasa.com/docs/rasa/nlg`.

In the next section, we will talk about how to control conversational sessions.

Configuring sessions

The session is a conversation between the user and the bot. One session can persist for multiple dialogue turns. Currently, Rasa supports two types of session configurations:

- `session_expiration_time` defines the expiration time (in minutes) after the user gets the newest message. There is no expiration time if it is set to 0.

- `carry_over_slots_to_new_session` defines whether the system should bring the slots from the previous session into the new session. If set to `false`, the new session will not get the slot values from the previous session.

Here is a configuration example:

```
session_config:
  session_expiration_time: 60
  carry_over_slots_to_new_session: true
```

Besides `session_config`, Rasa also has a global configuration item called `store_entities_as_slots`. It decides when the system gets NLU results, and whether it will synchronize the value to a slot with the same name. The default value is `true`.

We have now discussed the domain, its function, and configuration. In the next section, we will talk about a new concept – the story.

Training data for dialogue management (stories)

Rasa learns from conversations and manages knowledge by training on stories. The story is a high-level semantic way of recording conversations. It records not only the expressions from users, but also the correct state change within the system.

Rasa uses YAML format to store `stories`. Here is an example of a `story`:

```
stories:
  - story: This is the description of one story
    steps:
      - intent: greet
      - action: action_ask_howcanhelp
      - slot_was_set:
          - asked_for_help: true
      - intent: inform
        entities:
          - location: "New York"
          - price: "cheap"
      - action: action_on_it
      - action: action_ask_cuisine
```

```
- intent: inform
  entities:
    - cuisine: "Italian"
- action: restaurant_form
- active_loop: restaurant_form
```

Each story is an element of the `stories` list.

The story is a dictionary in the data structure. A valid story has at least two mandatory fields: `story` and `steps`. The `story` field records the summary of the story (the developer's description of the plot of the story). In this example, the description of the story is `This is the description of one story`. The other field is the `steps` field. This is used to record the steps of the story. The `steps` field is a list and linearly records the conversation flow between user and machine. Every time the user sends a message, the bot will execute one more series of tasks, and then wait for the user's new input (not reflected in the story). The user sends a message again and the flow goes on. In this way, steps actually consist of alternative information on the user's messages and the machine's actions.

Let's discuss the user's messages first.

User messages

User messages save the intent and entity information from the users. The format is as follows:

```
- intent: inform
  entities:
    - location: "New York"
    - price: "cheap"
```

In this example, `intent` gives the intent information, and `entities` gives the information of multiple entities. The entity with the `location` type has the `New York` value, and the entity with the `price` type has the `cheap` value.

Now we have covered the user's part of the story. In the next section, we will discuss the machine's part of the story.

Bot actions and events

When the dialogue management system is trained and tested, Rasa will not be able to execute the corresponding actions, so developers will not be able to get the output of the actions (represented as events). Thus, developers need to clearly define them in the story. The bot action includes what the action is and what event the action returns.

Bot actions are simply represented in YAML. An example is as follows:

```
- action: action_ask_howcanhelp
```

Here, `action_ask_howcanhelp` is the bot action.

For complex stories, there can be multiple actions from Rasa after one user request. For example, refer to the following:

```
- action: action_on_it
- action: action_ask_cuisine
```

For built-in actions, Rasa can automatically alter the state change-related information in the downstream processing, according to action types. However, Rasa cannot confirm the state change for customized actions during the training process. Developers need to manually define the state change. This kind of state change is called an event. Common events include slot events and loop events.

A slot event is an event that can make changes to the slot state. For example, refer to the following:

```
- slot_was_set:
- asked_for_help: true
```

Here, the slot of `asked_for_help` is set to be `true`.

A loop event is an event that can be activated or deactivated. For example, refer to the following:

```
- active_loop: restaurant_form
```

Here, the loop of `restaurant_form` is activated.

In order to make it easier for users to write stories, Rasa provides some useful features. In the next section, we will talk about them.

Auxiliary features (checkpoints and OR statements)

To support users to efficiently express complicated information within stories, Rasa provides two auxiliary features: **checkpoints** and **OR** statements. Let's start by looking at checkpoints.

Checkpoints

Checkpoints are used to reduce the repetitive parts in a story. Checkpoints with the same name can switch to each other. For example, refer to the following:

```
stories:
  - story: Process starts
    steps:
      - intent: greet
      - action: action_ask_user_question
      - checkpoint: check_asked_question
  - story: Handle user's confirmation
    steps:
      - checkpoint: check_asked_question
      - intent: affirm
      - action: action_handle_affirmation
      - checkpoint: check_flow_finished
  - story: Handle user's denial
    steps:
      - checkpoint: check_asked_question
      - intent: deny
      - action: action_handle_denial
      - checkpoint: check_flow_finished
  - story: Process ends
    steps:
      - checkpoint: check_flow_finished
      - intent: goodbye
      - action: utter_goodbye
```

A checkpoint at the end of one story can be linked to another checkpoint with the same name at the start of another story to form a new story. Here, the `Process starts` story can be linked to the `Handle user's confirmation` and the `Handle user's denial` story through the `check_asked_question` checkpoint. In this way, we form two new stories, and those two new stories can be linked to the `Process ends` story through the `check_flow_finished` checkpoint to form another new story.

We can see from the example that using checkpoints can reduce the repetitive work required for composing similar stories. However, we should not overuse checkpoints. Otherwise, our stories will be difficult to read, and their logic will be difficult to interpret by developers.

Next, we will talk about another helper feature: the OR statement.

OR statements

Sometimes two stories only differ on one specific conversation point. We do not want to write two almost identical stories just for this small difference. Otherwise, it will be difficult to maintain the stories afterward. We can use an OR expression to simplify the stories, as follows:

```
stories:
- story:
  steps:
    # ... previous steps
    - action: utter_ask_confirm
    - or:
        - intent: affirm
        - intent: thankyou
    - action: action_handle_affirmation
```

Here, we actually generate two stories with an OR expression. Those two stories are the same, except that in a single step, one story has its user intent as `affirm` and the other story has its user intent as `thankyou`.

In the next section, we will introduce the augmentation of stories.

Data augmentation (creating longer stories automatically)

In machine learning, a lack of sufficient data is a common problem, especially in NLP. To solve this issue, Rasa by default will connect (glue) multiple stories to create a new story. This is known as data augmentation for stories. Developers can use the `–augmentation` flag to set the data augmentation factor when running Rasa commands. Rasa will augment stories by 10 times the augmentation factor. Setting `–augmentation 0` will disable all the data augmentation behavior. For a more detailed explanation, please visit the official documentation at the following URL: `https://rasa.com/docs/rasa/2.0.x/policies#data-augmentation`.

Now, as we already understand the structure of stories, in the next section, we will talk about how a bot replies to or calls a third-party service API for users.

Reacting to user input (action)

The action receives user input and the conversation state and processes these according to business logic. It outputs events that change the conversation state and messages to reply to the user. There are four types of actions: **response actions**, **form actions**, **built-in actions**, and **custom actions**. Let's start with the simplest: response actions.

Response actions

This type of action is linked to the responses in the domain. When this type of action is called, the system will automatically search for the same name templates within the responses and render them. Since response actions need to have the same name with their responses, they need to start with `utter_`.

In the next section, we will talk about form actions.

Form actions

One important mode for task-oriented conversation is to continuously interact with users and collect elements that are needed by the tasks until the required information is complete. This mode is usually referred to as **forms**. Forms are particularly important, and we will discuss them in detail later.

In the next section, we will give you a brief introduction to built-in actions.

Built-in actions

Rasa provides developers with default actions for common and business independent actions, as follows:

Name	Function
action_ listen	Stop predicting actions and wait for user input.
action_ restart	Restart the conversation and clean the chat history and slot information. Users can input /restart in the channel to run this action.
action_ session_ start	All conversations run this action before starting to initiate the process. When the user's inactive time exceeds session_expiration_ time (configured in the domain file), this action will copy all the slots into a new session. Similar to action_restart, users can run / session_start to run this action.
action_ default_ fallback	Reset system state to the previous round (as if the user had never inputted the current message and the system had never responded), and call utter_default to send the user a message.
action_ deactivate_ loop	Stop the activated loop and reset the requested_slot slot.
action_ two_stage_ fallback	Trigger fallback logic when the NLU score is lower than a certain threshold.
action_ default_ask_ affirmation	Used by action_two_stage_fallback to ask the user to confirm their intent.
action_ default_ask_ rephrase	Used by action_two_stage_fallback to ask the user to rephrase their input.
action_back	Go back one round to the time before the latest user input. The user can input /back to run this action.

Figure 3.1 – Built-in actions

Note that those default actions can be replaced by custom actions with the same name. Next, we will talk about how to build your own actions.

Custom actions

Most conversational tasks require developers to customize their actions. Custom actions are implemented by developers to fulfill all kinds of backend communication and computational requirements. The most common backend communication is to query a database or call a third-party API.

For practical purposes to fulfill a real industrial need, Rasa custom actions are designed to provide an independent interface for developers to implement services. Those services interact with Rasa through the HTTP interface, so the development of services can be in any language. Rasa also provides developers with Rasa SDK to help Python developers develop custom action servers efficiently. We will cover custom actions later in this chapter.

Now that we have learned how a bot can react to the user's input via actions, in the next section, let's talk about the bot's memory elements: slots.

Understanding the memory of your bot (slots)

The slot is the memory of the chatbot. The slot is represented as a key-value pair, such as `city: New York`. It records the key information from conversations. The key information can come from a user's input (intents and entities), or from backend systems (for example, the result from a payment action: success or failure). Normally, the information is crucial for the flow of the conversation and will be used by the dialogue management system to predict the next action.

Let's take an example. In a simple application of a weather forecast, the information of location and date is key for the dialogue management system to decide the next action. If the system finds either the location or date missing, it will ask users for the corresponding information until both are present. Then the system will start to query some weather APIs.

Here, the system only cares about whether the location and date slots are filled. It does not care about the specific values in those slots, and those values will not affect predicting the next action. However, in another context, a different slot value may have a crucial impact on predicting the next action. For example, it may impact whether a payment is successful or not.

A slot must have a name and a type. For example, refer to the following:

```
slots:
  slot_name:
    type: text
```

This is a slot named `slot_name`, and its type is `text`.

Now we know how to define slots, in the next section, let's learn the function of slots.

The influences of slots on the conversation

In the configuration of a slot, the developer can set the `influence_conversation` flag to `true` or `false`, to make the slot affect the conversation or not. The `influence_conversation` bool configuration has a default value of `true`. When it is set as `false`, the slot is only used for storing information and will not influence the conversation behavior.

Here is an example:

```
slots:
  age:
    type: text
    influence_conversation: false
```

Here, the slot named `age` will not influence the conversation behavior. Different types of slots have different functions in a bot's memory. In the next section, we will discuss slot types.

Slot types

Each slot must have a type. The slot type decides how the system handles the slot value, so developers should choose the slot type very carefully.

Slots can have the following types:

- `text`: The `text` slot can store text values. Rasa does not care about the value content, so this type of slot is good for storing common entities.

- `bool`: The `bool` slot can only store `True` or `False` values. It is good for handling signals (for example, signals for whether a payment is successful or not).

- `category`: The `category` slot can only store predefined limited values (similar to the enumerated value in programming languages). Note that Rasa will add an extra *other* value to the predefined category values. When a specific value is assigned to the `category` slot, if it does not match any of the predefined category values, it will be assigned as *other*. A `category` slot is good for storing limited categorical values, such as gender and marital status. Rasa will use the slot values (converted to one-hot encodings) as part of features to predict the next actions.

- `float`: The `float` slot can store float numbers. A maximum value and a minimum value need to be defined. If the input value is out of range, it will be set as the maximum or minimum value. Rasa will use the slot value as part of features to predict actions.

- `list`: The `list` slot can store multiple values. Rasa only considers whether the list is empty or not as part of its features to predict the next action. The number of elements and the element values will not affect action prediction.

- `any`: The any slot has no effect on Rasa's action prediction. Developers can put values here that are not relevant to the system state for information transferring purposes.

In the next section, we will talk about how to connect slots with entities.

Automatic slot filling

In many cases, the slot value is given by the entity value. Rasa, by default, will assign the entity value generated from an NLU module to the slot with the same name as that entity. The developer can add `auto_fill: False` in the slot configuration to turn off this feature.

Next, we will talk about how to set initial values for slots.

Setting initial values for slots

A slot can be configured with customized initial values. If we want to set the slot `name` value to `human` as the initial value, we can do the following:

```
slots:
  name:
    type: text
    initial_value: "human"
```

We have learned about the function of slots and how to define slots. In the next section, we will discuss how bots make decisions.

Understanding the decision-maker of your bot (policies)

The policy method learns from stories and predicts the next actions.

Policies need to use a **featurizer** to convert stories into conversational states, get the state features, and use those features to predict the next action.

In Rasa, we can have multiple policies. Policies are trained independently and can be used together for final prediction according to their priorities and confidence scores.

Let's start with policy configuration.

Configuring policies

Policy configuration is done in the `config.yaml` file within a Rasa project. The part with key `policies` is reserved for policy configuration. Here is an example:

```
policies:
  - name: "MemoizationPolicy"
    max_history: 5
  - name: "FallbackPolicy"
    nlu_threshold: 0.4
    core_threshold: 0.3
    fallback_action_name: "my_fallback_action"
  - name: "path.to.your.policy.class"
    arg1: "..."
```

The configuration of a policy is similar to the pipeline configuration of the NLU module. It consists of several lists. Within each list, one element is a dictionary. The dictionary contains `name` as the component name, and the rest of the elements are configuration items.

As a powerful framework, Rasa has some built-in policies. In the next section, we will talk about them.

Built-in policies

Here, we will give brief introductions to Rasa's built-in policies. Users should pay attention to these policies because they are very important in dialogue management:

- `TEDPolicy`: **TED** stands for **Transformer Embedding Dialogue**. It is a set of dialogue prediction algorithms developed by Rasa. It uses transformer-based embeddings to convert the current dialogue into a dialogue vector and searches for the closest dialogue vector from existing actions.

- `MemoizationPolicy`: This is a simple policy that directly remembers the states and corresponding actions and records them into a dictionary. In the prediction step, the policy will directly look for the corresponding action for the specific state in the dictionary. If no state is found, it will fail.

- `AugmentedMemoizationPolicy`: This is `MemoizationPolicy` with a forgetting mechanism that will randomly forget a certain number of steps in the conversation history and try to find a match in stories with the reduced history.

- `RulePolicy`: This policy is rule-based. It combines all the rule-based policies in Rasa 1.x, including `MappingPolicy`, `FallbackPolicy`, `TwoStageFallbackPolicy`, and `FormPolicy`.

Generally, users only need to use the built-in policies. However, due to the complexity of developing custom policies, this is generally not recommended. In the next section, we will introduce how Rasa uses multiple policies to make decisions.

Policy priority

In Rasa, each policy independently makes a prediction for the next action, and the action with the highest confidence score is used (or in some cases, given higher weight for an ensemble decision). When scores are the same (in most cases, all get the highest score, 1), policy priority activates to decide what policy to use. The higher the priority score a policy has, the higher priority the policy gets. Rasa has a default policy priority setting that, in general, gives the most reasonable results:

Policy Priority	Policy
6	FormPolicy
3	MemoizationPolicy and AugmentedMemoizationPolicy
1	TEDPolicy

Figure 3.2 – Priorities of built-in policies

Note that although the policy priority score of both built-in and custom components can be configured by the key on priority, it is not recommended to modify the built-in policy priorities unless developers completely understand Rasa's source code. There are some implementations within Rasa that rely on the default priorities. Modifying them may cause unknown errors.

So far, we have discussed how Rasa works internally. In the next section, we will discuss how Rasa collaborates with external services.

Connecting with other services via endpoints

As a mature dialogue system, Rasa supports communication with external services and internal components in a similar way to microservices. In Rasa's terminology, all links to these services are called endpoints. The endpoint is the connection between Rasa Core and other services and is defined in `endpoints.yml`. Currently, the supported endpoints are as follows:

- **Event broker**: This allows you to connect your bot to other services that can process conversation data asynchronously. The event broker publishes messages to a message broker in order to forward conversations from Rasa to external services. This is useful for advanced users who want to analyze the conversations.

- **Tracker store**: Rasa's conversations are stored within a tracker store. Rasa provides several built-in tracker stores. In general, all tracker stores can be divided into two categories: the tracker store that is exclusive to the process and the tracker store that is globally shared outside the process. The former does not require the support of any external services but cannot achieve multi-instance concurrency. The latter needs to configure the corresponding third-party service but can achieve multi-instance concurrency.

- **Lock store**: This is a lock mechanism used by Rasa to ensure that messages for given users are always processed in the right order. This is a prerequisite for multi-instance concurrency in Rasa.

- **Action server**: This runs custom actions for Rasa. All the custom actions must be implemented in an action server. We will discuss this in detail in the next section.

- **NLG server**: This is the external alternative for generating a response, instead of using a built-in template-based response. This was already discussed in the section detailing responses.

- **Models server**: This allows Rasa to dynamically retrieve model files from other servers. Therefore, using this allows deployment in the production environment to become more efficient.

The action server and NLU server both have default configuration values that work very well. The developer may not need to configure them if used on a single machine. We will continue to discuss tracker store, lock store, and models server in *Chapter 9, Testing and Production Deployment*.

So far, we have examined all the elements needed for training. But before our bot can provide services to customers, we still need to complete a coding job. This will be to implement all custom actions.

Building custom actions using Rasa SDK

Custom actions provide a mechanism to run specific actions in remote servers. This is crucial for building a chatbot, as it is the gateway for implementing detailed business logic.

Installing the Rasa SDK package

Rasa integrates `rasa-sdk` in its package. So, when you install Rasa, it will also automatically install `rasa-sdk`. If we want to use `rasa-sdk` alone (for example, in a production environment), we can run the following command:

```
pip install rasa-sdk
```

Writing custom actions

Custom actions must inherit the `Action` class from the SDK, so that the server can automatically discover and register the custom actions. Here is an example:

```
from rasa_sdk import Action
from rasa_sdk.events import SlotSet


class ActionCheckRestaurants(Action):
    def name(self) -> Text:
        return "action_check_restaurants"


    def run(self,
            dispatcher: CollectingDispatcher,
            tracker: Tracker,
            domain: Dict[Text, Any]) -> List[Dict[Text, Any]]:

        cuisine = tracker.get_slot('cuisine')
        q = "select * from restaurants where cuisine='{0}' limit
1".format(cuisine)
        result = db.query(q)


        return [SlotSet("matches", result if result is not None
else [])]
```

By overriding the name method to return a string, we input the name of the action. By overriding the run method, we can get the current dialogue information (tracker and domain) and the dialogue interface (dispatcher) and use this information to complete the user's action. If we want to make a change to the current dialogue state (for example, changing the slot information), we will need to return one event or multiple events. If there is no change to the dialogue state, we still need to return an empty list.

You should have noticed that the run method of a custom action has three parameters: dispatcher, tracker, and domain. Among them, the most important parameter is tracker. This represents the tracking status of the current conversation. Next, we will introduce tracker objects in detail.

Tracker objects (tracking the states of conversations)

A tracker object represents the tracking of the dialogue state, namely the historical memory of the conversation. In custom actions, developers can use the tracker object to get the current (or history) dialogue state (entities, slot), and in most cases, input this into business logic.

Tracker objects have the following attributes:

Attribute	Description
sender_id	String type, representing the unique ID of the current interacting user
slots	List type, list of slots
latest_message	Dictionary type, including three keys: intent, entities, and text (user's message)
events	All events in the dialogue history
active_form	String type, representing the current activated form (can be empty meaning that no form is activated at the moment)
latest_action_name	String type, representing the name of the latest action

Figure 3.3 – Attributes of tracker objects

`Tracker` objects have the following methods:

Method	Description
`current_state()`	Return the current tracker object.
`is_paused()`	Return whether the current tracker is paused or not.
`get_latest_entity_values()`	Return the latest value of an entity.
`get_latest_input_channel()`	Return the name of the latest input channel the user used.
`events_after_latest_restart()`	Return all the events from the last restart.
`get_slot()`	Return the value of a slot.

Figure 3.4 – Methods of tracker objects

So far, we have learned about `tracker` objects. A `tracker` object is the most important input parameter for an action. Now it is time to talk about the outputs of an action: event objects.

Event objects (records for changes in conversations)

An event object is used when we want to change the dialogue state in a custom action.

Here are the common event objects:

Event object	Description
`SlotSet(key, value=None)`	Set value for the slot with the target key.
`Restarted()`	Restart the dialogue process.
`AllSlotReset()`	Reset all slots.
`ReminderScheduled()`	Initiate a request at a given time with a given intent and entities.
`ReminderCancelled()`	Cancel a scheduled reminder.
`ConversationPaused()`	Pause the dialogue process.
`ConversationResumed()`	Resume the dialogue process.
`FollowupAction(name)`	Force to set the next action (instead of getting the next action from a prediction).

Figure 3.5 – Common event objects

The following is a list of the automatic tracking events (created by the system):

Event Object	Description
UserUttered()	Representing a user's input message.
BotUttered()	Representing the message, a bot sends to the user.
UserUtteranceReverted()	Cancel all the events (including user events) that happen after the user's last message (UserUttered). Normally, only action_listen is left, and the bot reverts to the state of waiting for the user's input.
ActionReverted()	Cancel the last action, clear all the event effects from the last action, and the bot will revert to predicting the next action.
ActionExecuted()	Record an action (the event created by the action will be recorded separately).
SessionStarted()	Start a new dialogue session, reset the tracker, and trigger ActionSessionStart (by default this will copy the existing slots to the new session).

Figure 3.6 – Event objects created by Rasa

We already know how to create custom actions. The last piece of the puzzle when building custom actions is to know how to set them up so that Rasa can access them. This is the central topic of the next section.

Running custom actions

If custom action is a part of the Rasa package, we can run the following:

```
rasa run actions
```

If the custom action is from the independent SDK, we can run the following:

```
python -m rasa_sdk --actions actions
```

In the next section, we will discuss how to configure Rasa so that it can communicate with other software.

Using channels to communicate with instant messaging software

In most cases, users will be using all kinds of **instant messaging** (**IM**) apps to interact with chatbots.

Rasa is one of the best platforms for seamlessly integrating with different IMs. Rasa supports most of the mainstream IMs on the market that support OpenAPI. Currently, it includes Facebook Messenger, Slack, Telegram, Twilio, Microsoft Bot Framework, Cisco Webex Teams, RocketChat, Mattermost, and Google Hangouts Chat.

Community developers have also developed many open source IMs for Rasa, and those open source IMs are often used by start-ups and developers for product demonstration purposes. Rasa Webchat (`https://github.com/botfront/rasa-webchat`) and Chatroom (`https://github.com/scalableminds/chatroom`) have the most mature functionalities.

In Rasa, the connector is responsible for connecting a Rasa system to an IM. The Connect feature handles the communication protocol. Since different IMs may share the same communication protocol, one connector may serve multiple IMs. All of the previously outlined IMs have their own version of a connector.

Rasa also supports custom connectors for developers to connect to other non-listed IMs. Rasa supports using multiple connecters simultaneously in order to connect to multiple IMs. Developers need to configure them in a `credentials.yml` file.

Rasa has detailed documentation for all the connectors. Here is a configuration example for Rasa Webchat:

```
socketio:
    user_message_evt: user_uttered
    bot_message_evt: bot_uttered
    session_persistence: false
```

Note that `socketio` is used here because `socketio` is the underlying protocol for Rasa Webchat.

So far, we have learned about all the parts of Rasa Core. In the next section, we will do some hands-on exercises.

Building a tell-the-time bot

A tell-the-time bot is one of the most basic and simplest chatbots. It is very suitable as an introductory exercise project, allowing learners to understand what each part of the Rasa system does. All the project files can be found under the directory named ch03 in the GitHub repository, available at the following URL: https://github.com/PacktPublishing/Conversational-AI-with-RASA. Let's start by outlining the target functions this bot should provide.

Defining the features that our bot should provide

In this section, we will list all the functions this exercise project should provide. Let's start with greetings and goodbyes.

Handling greetings and goodbyes

Example #1: The bot responds to the user's greeting, as follows:

```
User: Hello!
Bot: Hello, my name is Silly. I can help you get the time and
date. You may ask me "What time is it?", "What's the date
today?" or "What day is it tomorrow?".
```

Example #2: The bot echoes goodbye to the user, as follows:

```
User: Bye bye!
Bot: Goodbye!
```

Asking for a time

Example: The user asks for the current time, as follows:

```
User: What time is it now?
Bot: It's 12:27 PM.
```

Asking for a date

Example #1: The user asks for the current date, as follows:

```
User: What's the date today?
Bot: It's March 25, 2021.
```

Example #2: The user asks for a future date, as follows:

```
User: What's the date tomorrow?
Bot: It's March 26, 2021.
```

Example #3: The user asks for a past date, as follows:

```
User: What was the date yesterday?
Bot: It's March 24, 2021.
```

Since it is impossible to convert all possible text representing the date (for example, tomorrow, Christmas, 5 days ago) to the absolute date (Unix timestamp), our bot needs to remind users in a friendly way that this is beyond the bot's understanding. The bot should have no response or directly give users technical errors.

Example #4: A friendly reminder if the user asks a question that is beyond the bot's understanding, as follows:

```
User: What's the date for Chinese New Year?
Bot: Sorry, we don't yet support date for "Chinese New Year".
```

Asking for a weekday

Example #1: The user asks for the current weekday, as follows:

```
User: What day is it today?
Bot: Thursday.
```

Example #2: The user asks for a past or future weekday, as follows:

```
User: What day is it tomorrow?
Bot: Friday.
```

Similar to asking for a date, we should also have exception handling for asking for the weekday.

In this section, we covered all the functions this bot should provide. In the next section, we will learn how to implement such functions file by file.

How can we implement those features?

Our project follows the Rasa official project structure, detailed as follows:

```
.
├── actions
│   ├── actions.py
│   └── __init__.py
├── config.yml
├── credentials.yml
├── data
│   ├── nlu.yml
│   └── stories.yml
├── domain.yml
├── endpoints.yml
└── tests
```

In this project, `actions/__init__.py` and `credentials.yml` are empty. Here we will introduce the content of the rest of the files.

Let's start with the NLU training file.

Defining the NLU training data

In the NLU training data file, we have training data for five intents: `greet`, `goodbye`, `query_time`, `query_date`, and `query_weekday`. In that training data, we have one entity: `date`. We can easily infer the meaning from the intent's name and the entity name. In our project, all the training data is stored in the `data/nlu.yml` file. Here, we will show you part of the training file (the full content has already been provided to you at `https://github.com/PacktPublishing/Conversational-AI-with-RASA/blob/main/Chapter03/data/nlu.yml`) to help you gain a better understanding of the training data:

```
version: "2.0"
nlu:
  - intent: greet
    examples:
      - Hello
      - hi
  - intent: goodbye
```

```yaml
    examples:
      - ByeBye
      - bye
  - intent: query_time
    examples:
      - What's the time now
      - What time it is
  - intent: query_date
    examples:
      - What's the date [today](date)
      - What's the date of [tomorrow](date)
  - intent: query_weekday
    examples:
      - What day is [today](date)
      - The day of the week
```

In the next section, we will talk about the story training data.

Defining story data

The story data file contains stories. In this project, our stories are very forthright. Every intent will trigger its related action. Specifically, the greet intent will trigger the utter_ greet action, the goodbye intent will trigger the utter_goodbye action, the query_ time intent will trigger the action_query_time action, the query_date intent will trigger the action_query_date action, and the query_weekday intent will trigger the action_query_weekday action. The entire contents of data/stories.yml are as follows:

```yaml
version: "2.0"
stories:
  - story: say greet
    steps:
      - intent: greet
      - action: utter_greet
  - story: query time
    steps:
      - intent: query_time
      - action: action_query_time
```

```
- story: query date
  steps:
    - intent: query_date
    - action: action_query_date
- story: query weekday
  steps:
    - intent: query_weekday
    - action: action_query_weekday
- story: say goodbye
  steps:
    - intent: goodbye
    - action: utter_goodbye
```

In the next section, we will talk about domain settings.

Configuring domain settings

The domain.yml file contains Rasa's domain settings. For this project, our domain settings contain all the intents, entities, actions, and responses. We also added a date slot to remember date information. This slot has the same name as the date entity. This design can use the autofill feature of the slot. The full contents of domain.yml are as follows:

```
version: "2.0"
session_config:
  session_expiration_time: 60
  carry_over_slots_to_new_session: true
intents:
  - greet
  - goodbye
  - query_time
  - query_date
  - query_weekday
entities:
  - date
slots:
  date:
    type: any
```

```
responses:
  utter_greet:
    - text: Hello, I'm Silly, I can check the time, date and
day of the week for you. You can ask me "what time is it now?",
"what day is today?" or "what day is tomorrow?"
  utter_goodbye:
    - text: Goodbye!
actions:
  - action_query_time
  - action_query_date
  - action_query_weekday
  - utter_goodbye
  - utter_greet
```

In the next section, we will talk about NLU pipeline settings.

Configuring the pipeline and policies

Configurations of Rasa are stored in the config.yml file. In the NLU part, we use transformer-based components to classify intents and extract entities. In the policy part, we use MemoizationPolicy and TEDPolicy. The full contents of config.yml are as follows:

```
language: en
pipeline:
  - name: WhitespaceTokenizer
  - name: LanguageModelFeaturizer
    model_name: "bert"
    model_weights: "rasa/LaBSE"
  - name: DIETClassifier
    epochs: 100
    learning_rate: 0.001
policies:
  - name: MemoizationPolicy
  - name: TEDPolicy
    max_history: 5
    epochs: 100
```

In the next section, we will talk about endpoint settings.

Configuring endpoints

The endpoints.yml file contains Rasa's endpoint settings. For this project, we only have one endpoint that needs to be specified: action_endpoint. By default, the Rasa action server will listen to port 5055. Generally, we run the Rasa server and the Rasa action server on the same machine. So, generally, the action_endpoint endpoint is set to http://localhost:5055/webhook. The full content of endpoints.yml is as follows:

```
action_endpoint:
  url: "http://localhost:5055/webhook"
```

In the next section, we will talk about custom actions.

Writing your own custom actions

All of the custom actions are defined in the actions/actions.py file. In this project, we will define three custom actions: action_query_time, action_query_date, and action_query_weekday.

In this section, we will only show the key code snippets. To view the full code, please visit our GitHub repository at the following URL: https://github.com/PacktPublishing/Conversational-AI-with-RASA.

Let's start with action_query_time.

Action (action_query_time)

The action_query_time action takes no inputs and outputs the current time to the user. Its implementation code is as follows:

```
class ActionQueryTime(Action):
    def name(self):
        return "action_query_time"


    def run(self, dispatcher, tracker, domain):
        current_time = datetime.now().strftime("It's %H:%M
%p.")
        dispatcher.utter_message(text=current_time)
        return []
```

In the code, we first get the current time by using `datetime.now()`. `strftime("%H:%M:%S")`, and then send the time information to the user by calling `dispatcher.utter_message()`.

Action (action_query_date)

The `action_query_date` action takes the `date` slot as the input and outputs date information according to the `date` slot. Its implementation code is as follows:

```
class ActionQueryDate(Action):
    def name(self):
        return "action_query_date"

    def run(self, dispatcher, tracker, domain):
        text_date = tracker.get_slot("date") or "today"
        int_date = text_date_to_int(text_date)
        if int_date is not None:
            delta = timedelta(days=int_date)
            current_date = datetime.now()
            target_date = current_date + delta
            dispatcher.utter_message(
                text=target_date.strftime("It's %B %d, %Y.")
            )
        else:
            dispatcher.utter_message(
                text="The system currently doesn't support date
 query for '{}'".format(text_date)
            )
        return []
```

In the code, we will try to get the value of the slot named `date`. If it is `None`, it means that the user did not specify a date. We would then use `today` as the default value. Then we try to parse the value to a number that represents the offset days to today (0 means today, 1 means tomorrow, 2 means the day after tomorrow). If the parsing fails, we send a message to tell users that we currently do not support such a query. If the parsing succeeds, we will translate the offset information to date information, and send it to users.

Action (action_query_weekday)

The `action_query_weekday` action takes the `date` slot as the input and outputs the weekday information according to the `date` slot. Its implementation code is as follows:

```
class ActionQueryWeekday(Action):
    def name(self):
        return "action_query_weekday"

    def run(self, dispatcher, tracker, domain):
        text_date = tracker.get_slot("date") or "today"

        int_date = text_date_to_int(text_date)
        if int_date is not None:
            delta = timedelta(days=int_date)
            current_date = datetime.now()
            target_date = current_date + delta
            dispatcher.utter_message(
                text=weekday_to_text(target_date.weekday()))
        else:
            dispatcher.utter_message(
                text="The system currently doesn't support day
of week query for '{}'".format(
                    text_date)
            )
        return []
```

The implementation of `action_query_weekday` is very similar to `action_query_date`. The only difference is that `action_query_weekday` outputs a weekday, while `action_query_date` outputs a date.

With all those files in place, we can start to train a Rasa model.

Training models, serving models, and making inferences

In this section, we will cover how to train a model, how to serve it, and how to make inferences. Let's start with training a Rasa model.

Training Rasa models

Because we followed Rasa's standard project structure, we can use Rasa's built-in command-line tools to perform various tasks. Of course, training a new model is one of those tasks.

Users should open the terminal application in their operating systems. First, change the working directory to the current Rasa project directory (in most operating systems, the command that changes the working directory is cd). Second, type the following command and execute it:

```
rasa train
```

After waiting for few minutes, the training will be done. There will be a model automatically saved as a zipped file in the models folder.

The next step will be to start an action server that provides custom actions for the Rasa server.

Running the action server

Open a terminal application, change it to the current Rasa project directory, then type the following command to start an action server:

```
rasa run actions
```

Since this is a server, the command will not exit. It will continue running.

In the next section, we will start a Rasa server and use a client to make some inferences.

Running the Rasa server and client

To simplify the configuration, we use Rasa's built-in shell client for this project.

When the Rasa shell starts, it will also start a Rasa server. To run a Rasa server, we need to open another terminal application instance, then type the following command:

```
rasa shell
```

After the loading is complete, we can now interact with the bot in the shell command line:

```
Your input -> What time is it now?
It's 18:21 PM.
```

Congratulations! You have completed all the steps and successfully built a tell-the-time robot.

Summary

In this chapter, we discussed Rasa Core. This is the dialogue management part of Rasa. You should now have a good understanding of how to define all the key concepts for Rasa Core: domain, response, story, action, slot, and policy. You should also have a good understanding of how to use Rasa SDK to develop your own custom actions, and how to connect Rasa Core with IM software and use Rasa to develop simple chatbots.

In the next chapter, we will take a deeper look at how to handle business logic effectively in Rasa.

Section 2:
Rasa in Action

In this section, you will learn how to use the functions provided by the Rasa framework to build different types of chatbots. You will also learn how to create and use custom components. Through hands-on examples, you will gain practical experience in handling various dialogue tasks.

This section comprises the following chapters:

- *Chapter 4, Handling Business Logic*
- *Chapter 5, Working with Response Selector to Handle Chitchat and FAQs*
- *Chapter 6, Knowledge Base Actions to Handle Question Answering*
- *Chapter 7, Entity Roles and Groups for Complex Named Entity Recognition*
- *Chapter 8, Working Principles and Customization of Rasa*

4
Handling Business Logic

In this chapter, we will show you how to handle business logic. We will first introduce fallbacks that handle situations where the system cannot process users' needs. Then we will introduce the rule policy that uses predefined logic to select a fixed response. Finally, we will talk about the form where the essential information will automatically gather and execute related action. With all those functions, Rasa gives developers great flexibility in handling different business logic. By using these features, you should be able to handle complex business logic more elegantly and efficiently.

We will cover the following topics:

- The fallback mechanism in Rasa
- Making intents trigger actions
- Using forms to complete tasks
- Practice – building a weather forecast chatbot

Let's start with the fallback.

Technical requirements

You can find all the files for this chapter in the ch04 directory of the GitHub repository at https://github.com/PacktPublishing/Conversational-AI-with-RASA.

In the practice section of this chapter, we will use weather APIs from OpenWeather (https://openweathermap.org/). We should install the client library for OpenWeather APIs with the following command:

```
pip install pyowm
```

The fallback mechanism in Rasa

In real life, there will always be situations that chatbots cannot handle. For example, the user input voice is not clear enough, or the requested service is beyond what the system can offer. Then we need a fallback operation to handle those exceptions so that we can still elegantly reply to users with something like *Sorry, I could not understand what you meant*. Categorized by triggering cause, fallbacks can be NLU fallback or policy fallback.

Now, let's start with NLU fallback.

Handling fallback in NLU

NLU fallback is used to handle situations where the NLU module cannot clearly understand what user's intent is. The FallbackClassifier component is used for this purpose, and its configuration example is as follows:

```
pipeline:
  - name: FallbackClassifier
    threshold: 0.6
    ambiguity_threshold: 0.1
```

Here, if the confidence of the intent with the highest score is equal to or lower than 0.6 (specified by the threshold field), the intent will be replaced by nlu_fallback. Suppose the confidence difference between the top two intents is less than 0.1 (specified by the ambiguity_threshold field). In that case, the intent will also be replaced with nlu_fallback. Then we can set up a rule to map nlu_fallback to the action we prefer, for example:

```
rules:
  - rule: Ask user to speak again
    steps:
```

```
    - intent: nlu_fallback
    - action: utter_please_rephrase
```

Here, we map `nlu_fallback` to `utter_please_rephrase`, meaning that once `nlu_fallback` is triggered (system triggers NLU fallback condition), then the `utter_please_rephrase` action will be performed. The `utter_please_rephrase` action will render the template with the same name and the user can get the fallback message.

Rasa predefines `action_two_stage_fallback` to implement the two-stage fallback function. If needed, developers can also change the action mapping to `action_two_stage_fallback`.

In the next section, we will discuss another fallback: policy fallback.

Handling fallback in policy

Policy fallback is used when the predicted next action is not confident, or there are multiple best actions with very close confidence scores. To tackle this, we can use `RulePolicy` with options as shown in the following code block:

```
policies:
  - name: RulePolicy
    core_fallback_threshold: 0.3
    core_fallback_action_name: "action_default_fallback"
    enable_fallback_prediction: True
```

In this example, if all the actions predicted by the policy have a confidence score below or equal to `0.3` (set in `core_fallback_threshold`), then `action_default_fallback` is picked as the default action. By default, `action_default_fallback` will render the template named `utter_default` and return it to the user. To change this, developers can change the option in `core_fallback_action_name`.

In the next section, we will talk about how to make intents trigger actions.

Making intents trigger actions

In actual application scenarios, it is very useful to trigger the execution of specific actions by sending intents. Fortunately, Rasa provides support for triggering between intentions and actions. There are two types of trigger sources: built-in and user-defined.

Let's start by talking about the built-in triggers.

Triggering actions by using built-in intents

Rasa allows developers to use a format such as `/intent{"entity1": val1, "entity2": val2}` as a simplified way of defining intent and entities. We can use this to test the bot. Another usage is to return payload to the system when a user clicks on a button. This format is very similar to the user message in `story.md`; however, here it must start with `/`.

`RulePolicy` gives the corresponding intents `restat`, `back`, and `session_start` for the session-level actions `action_start`, `action_back`, and `action_session_start`, and manages the mapping from intent to action so that session-level control can be done when system gets the intents and triggers the corresponding actions.

As we mentioned before, Rasa supports a simplified way to define intents. Users can input `/restart`, `/back`, and `/session_start` to input the intents of `action_start`, `action_back`, and `action_session_start`, so that the system can map them to the corresponding actions.

In the next section, we will talk about the custom triggers.

Triggering actions by using custom intents

In some use cases, developers want to make sure that a certain intent will always trigger one or multiple actions no matter what dialogue state the system is in. In this situation, we can use the `rule` function within `RulePolicy`. It is configured in `stories.yml`:

```yaml
rules:
- rule: mapping from some_intent to some_action
  steps:
  - intent: some_intent
  - action: some_action
```

Here, if `RulePolicy` is initiated in the policy, when the user gets to the intent of `some_intent`, `RulePolicy` makes it certain that `some_action` is triggered.

In the next section, we will talk about how to use forms to finish tasks.

Using forms to complete tasks

A dialogue with the core target of completing a specific task can be considered as a process to guide users to fill in a form:

1. Bot asks user what he or she wants.

2. User expresses his or her need (with intent and entities).

3. Bot looks for the right form with regard to the user intent and fills in the entity information from user's input. If certain fields are still missing in the form, bot asks user about the missing field with a certain strategy (order of fields).

4. User provides bot with information on the missing fields.

5. Bot fills in the entity information to the form and continues to ask for the next missing field.

6. The process iterates until bot finds that the form is complete and starts to execute the specific task.

We need to add `RulePolicy` into the configuration file so that Rasa can handle dialogue management based on forms:

```
policies:
  - name: RulePolicy
```

Let's now start to discuss how to define a form.

Defining a form

A form in Rasa defines the information of all the slots required to perform the task of this form. We need to give a name to the form and list all its slots. Before we introduce every field we need to define, let me give you a sample form:

```
forms:
  weather_form:
    address:
      - entity: address
        type: from_entity
    date-time:
      - entity: date-time
        type: from_entity
```

In the sample form, all the form definitions are under the `forms` key. In this case, we only have one form, the name of the form is `weather_form`. The form defines two slots: `address` and `date_time`.

Sometimes, extracting slot value from an NLU parse result is complex. For example, you only want to use the value of a certain entity as the value of the slot when the intent is equal to a certain value and use the value of another entity when it is not. In order to help users more easily complete the work of extracting slot values from NLU parsing results, Rasa provides slot mapping functions in the form definition. The slot mapping specifies how to selectively extract the value of the slot from the NLU parsing result. Users can define multiple slot mapping settings. In this case, both slots only have one for each. The value of `type` of slot mapping is specific to the slot mapping type; in our case, it is `from_entity`. It means we will use the value of an entity as the slot's value, but which entity should we use? The `entity` key is used for specifying the source entity. Here, both of the slot values come from entities with the same name. Rasa offers many slot mapping solutions. Details can be found on Rasa's official documentation.

In the next section, we will talk about how to activate forms.

Activating a form

The easiest way to activate the form is to use the rule policy. We can use the rule policy to set such a rule: when a specific intent appears, the corresponding form will be automatically activated. Here is an example:

```
rules:
  - rule: activate form
    steps:
      - intent: weather
      - action: weather_form
      - active_loop: weather_form
```

In this example, if the user intent is `weather`, the action of `weather_form` will be performed. The side-effect of this action (change to the dialogue state) is to enter the `active_loop` named `weather_form`, the same as the form name we defined in the previous example. In this way, the system will go into the loop process of slot filling and enquiry.

In the next section, we will talk about how to use forms to execute actions.

Executing a form task

When all the slots requested by the form are filled, it is time to perform the form task (the action you want to perform with the information collected by these forms). We can use a rule to specify the settings we want. The following is an example:

```
- rule: submit form
    condition:
      # Condition that form is active.
      - active_loop: weather_form
    steps:
      - action: weather_form
      - active_loop: null
      - slot_was_set:
          - requested_slot: null
      # The action we want to run when the form is submitted.
      - action: action_weather_form_submit
```

Here, the rule defines that when the `active_loop` named `weather_form` is finished and all the requested slots are filled (here, `requested_slot: null`), the action `action_weather_form_submit` will be executed. All the business logic should be implemented within `action_weather_form_submit`. In this case, it will call a third-party API to get the weather information.

In the next section, let's do an exercise about what we have learned so far.

Practice – building a weather forecast chatbot

Here, we consolidate the knowledge we have learned so far and build a demo project on a chatbot that can forecast the weather.

Let's talk about the functions of this bot first.

Designing the features of this bot

The chatbot can give users a weather forecast according to the user's input on a city (Beijing, New York) and date (tomorrow, next Monday). We will use a form to implement those features.

In the next section, we will show you how to implement such a bot in great detail.

Implementing the bot step by step

Our project follows the Rasa official project structure, as shown in the following code block:

```
.
├── actions
│   ├── actions.py
│   └── __init__.py
├── config.yml
├── credentials.yml
├── data
│   ├── nlu.yml
│   └── stories.yml
├── domain.yml
├── endpoints.yml
└── tests
```

In this project, `actions/__init__.py` and `credentials.yml` are empty. We here introduce the content of the rest of the files.

Let's start with the NLU training file.

Defining NLU training data

In `data/nlu.yml`, we have training data for five intents: `greet`, `goodbye`, `weather`, `info_date`, and `info_address`. In addition, in that training data, we have entities: `date-time` and `address`.

We can easily understand the meaning from the intent name and the entity name. Part of the training data is as follows (the full content of this file has already been provided to you in the GitHub repository):

```
version: "2.0"
nlu:
  - intent: goodbye
    examples: |
      - Bye
      - Goodbye
  - intent: greet
    examples: |
```

```
        - Hello there
        - Hi
    - intent: weather
      examples: |
        - Display the weather in degrees Celsius
        - I want the weather of [Shanghai](address)[tomorrow]
(date-time)
    - intent: info_date
      examples: |
        - [Tomorrow] (date-time)
        - [The day after tomorrow](date-time)
    - intent: info_address
      examples: |
        - Tell me how about [Rome](address)
        - In [Seoul](address)
```

In the next section, let's talk about the settings of the domain.

Configuring the domain

The domain.yml file contains Rasa's domain setting. For this project, our domain
settings contain all the intents, entities, actions, and responses. We have also added the
slots date-time and address to remember date and city information. We define a
form (named weather_form) to do our weather query information collection job. Part
of the content of domain.yml is as follows (you can find the full content at https://
github.com/PacktPublishing/Conversational-AI-with-RASA//blob/
main/Chapter04/domain.yml):

```
intents:
    - goodbye
<-- we have omitted some similar items here. -->
entities:
    - address
    - date-time
<-- we have omitted the slots and responses field here. -->
actions:
    - utter_ask_address
<-- we have omitted some similar items here. -->
forms:
```

```
weather_form:
  address:
    - entity: address
      type: from_entity
  date-time:
    - entity: date-time
      type: from_entity
```

In the next section, we will discuss the dialogue management part of this project: stories and rules.

Defining stories and rules

The `data/stories.yml` file contains stories and rules. In this project, our stories are used to trigger the greet and say goodbye function. We already explained these settings in the previous chapter. Here is the concrete setting for the project:

```
version: "2.0"
stories:
  - story: greet
    steps:
      - intent: greet
      - action: utter_greet
  - story: say goodbye
    steps:
      - intent: goodbye
      - action: utter_goodbye
```

In another part, we will talk about rules. We use a rule to trigger the execution of form `weather_form` by intent `weather`. Specifically, when the user expresses the intent `weather`, our rule will activate the form `weather_form`. When all the required information is gathered (when `requested_slot: null`), our rule will trigger the running of `action_weather_form_submit`. The entire content of `data/stories.yml` is as follows:

```
rules:
  - rule: activate weather form
    steps:
      - intent: weather
      - action: weather_form
```

```
    - active_loop: weather_form
- rule: Submit form
  condition:
    # Condition that form is active.
    - active_loop: weather_form
  steps:
    - action: weather_form
    - active_loop: null
    - slot_was_set:
        - requested_slot: null
    # The action we want to run when the form is submitted.
    - action: action_weather_form_submit
```

In the next section, we will work on how to configure the pipeline and strategy.

Configuring the pipeline and strategy

The configurations of Rasa are stored in the `config.yml` file. In this project, we use transformer-based components to classify intent and extract entities. In the policy part, we use `MemoizationPolicy`, `TEDPolicy`, and `RulePolicy`. The full content of `config.yml` is as follows:

```
version: "2.0"
language: en
pipeline:
  - name: WhitespaceTokenizer
  - name: LanguageModelFeaturizer
    model_name: "bert"
    model_weights: "rasa/LaBSE"
  - name: RegexFeaturizer
  - name: DIETClassifier
    epochs: 100
    learning_rate: 0.001
  - name: ResponseSelector
    epochs: 100
    learning_rate: 0.001
  - name: EntitySynonymMapper
  - name: FallbackClassifier
```

```
policies:
  - name: MemoizationPolicy
  - name: TEDPolicy
    epochs: 100
  - name: RulePolicy
```

In the next section, we will talk about how to code our custom action for weather queries.

Creating a custom action

All the custom actions are defined in the `actions/actions.py` file. In this project, we will define only one action: `action_weather_form_submit`. This action is used to query weather conditions from a third-party service provider by using date and location information specified by users.

Now we will show the key code snippets for you. To view the full code, please visit our GitHub repository:

```
class ActionWeatherFormSubmit(Action):
    def name(self) -> Text:
        return "action_weather_form_submit"
    def run(self, dispatch, tracker, domain):
        city = tracker.get_slot("address")
        date_text = tracker.get_slot("date-time")
        date_object = text_to_date(date_text)
        if not date_object:  # parse date_time failed
            msg = "Not support weather query for {}".
format([city, date_text])
            dispatch.utter_message(msg)
        else:
            dispatch.utter_message(template="utter_working_on_
it")
            try:
                lat, lon = text_to_coordinate(city)
                weather_data = get_text_weather_date(lat, lon,
date_object, date_text, city)
            except Exception as e:
                exec_msg = str(e)
                dispatch.utter_message(exec_msg)
```

```
        else:
                dispatch.utter_message(weather_data)
        return []
```

In brief, this action will first try to parse the date information from the date-time slot (by using text_to_date()). Then it will try to parse the city information from the address slot. Finally (by using text_to_coordinate()), it will send a request to a third-party weather service provider to get the weather conditions (by using get_text_weather_date()) and send them to the user.

In the next section, we will discuss how to set up a web-based client for our project.

Setting up the web server for client UI

Normally, users interact with the Rasa server through a client. In this chapter, unlike previous chapters, we will not use the Rasa shell anymore; in this project, we will use a web-based client.

The web-based client has many advantages over the Rasa shell. For example, it is easier to distribute to users (as long as users have a web browser) and generally has richer response types (can display buttons and images sent from the Rasa server). More importantly, the Rasa shell can only be used for local tests. It cannot be used by other people who cannot access this computer physically. The web-based client is a production solution. If your users have web browsers, they can use your bot service. Of course, the Rasa shell certainly has its advantages. It can produce detailed logs, which is very handy for debugging. We will cover this feature in *Chapter 11, Debugging, Optimization and Community Ecosystem*.

The core code of the client is as follows:

```
<body>
  <div id="webchat"/>
  <script src="webchat.js"></script>
  <script>
      WebChat.default.init({
          selector: "#webchat",
          initPayload: "Hello",
          interval: 1000,
          customData: {"userId": "123"},
          socketUrl: "http://127.0.0.1:5005",
          socketPath: "/socket.io/",
          title: "Weather Forcasting",
```

```
        subtitle: "Demo",
        showCloseButton: true,
        fullScreenMode: false
    })
</script>
</body>
```

Here, we give you some explanations on the key parameters in the code:

- initPayload: When the user first opens the client, the client will send the value of this parameter (in our case, it is "Hello") as a message to Rasa. This message will not be shown in the user interface, so from the user's view, it seems that Rasa actively sends a message to users at the start.

- socketUrl: This parameter defines the address for the Rasa server.

- title: This parameter defines the main title of the chat window.

- subtitle: This parameter defines the subtitle of the chat window.

The webchat.js file loaded into the web page provides the JavaScript WebChat class. The file comes from the rasa-webchat project at https://github.com/botfront/rasa-webchat.

After loading the code, we will be able to get a chat widget in the lower-right corner of the web page, as shown in the following diagram:

Figure 4.1 – A chat widget located in the lower-right corner of the web page

In the next section, we will start to train the models.

Training models via the command line

Because we followed Rasa's standard project structure, we can use Rasa's built-in command-line tools to train models.

Users should open the terminal application of their operating systems. First, change the working directory to the current Rasa project directory (in most operating systems, the command that changes the working directory is cd). Second, type the following command and execute it:

```
rasa train
```

After waiting for a few minutes, the training will be done. There will be a model automatically saved as a zipped file in the models folder.

Now we have finished the training job, in the next section, we will run the whole dialogue system.

Running the dialogue system

For running the whole dialogue system, we need to run three separate servers: Rasa server, action server, and web client server. Let's see each of them in detail:

- Rasa server

  To run the server, use the following command:

```
rasa run --cors "*"
```

  The --cors "*" command is used to solve the **cross-origin resource sharing** (**CORS**) problem between client and Rasa servers.

- Action server

  We use a third-party weather forecasting API in this project, so we need to transfer the API key through the environment variable, as shown in the following command:

```
OWM_KEY=<your-owm-key> rasa run actions
```

  The <your-owm-key> key is the API key we can get from https://openweathermap.org/.

- Web client server

  Run the following command:

```
python -m http.server
```

This will start an HTTP-based server in the local 8000 port. We can visit `http://localhost:8000` in a browser to visit the chatbot.

In the next section, we will try to inspire you to do some cool things based on our current work.

Extending this project

A weather forecast chatbot is just a simple example as a start. When we understand this project better, we can add more features based on our needs. Here are some excellent examples:

- Using a custom **Natural Language Generation (NLG)** server to add `"Good Morning"`, `"Good Afternoon"`, and `"Good Evening"` according to the user's current time

- Using an event broker mechanism to calculate the distribution of different cities and dates from all the conversations generated from the chatbot users

Summary

In this chapter, we have introduced how to handle business logic. We first taught you how to use fallbacks to handle situations where the system cannot process a user's needs. Then we introduced the rule policy that can use predefined logic to execute a fixed action. Finally, we introduced forms that can automatically interact with users to gather the information that is needed by the task. We also built a weather forecast chatbot to help you understand those concepts better.

In the next chapter, we will discuss how to handle chitchat and FAQs.

5

Working with Response Selector to Handle Chitchat and FAQs

Most chatbots have simple FAQ and chitchat functions. Both types of functions involve knowing how to choose an appropriate response to a user's request. These functions sound simple, but in reality, they actually involve a lot of work. If we use one intent to represent an FAQ or chitchat intent from the user and pair it with an action, the story will become both complicated and inefficient. **Rasa** offers the **Natural Language Understanding** (NLU) ResponseSelector component, which is specifically used for FAQ and chitchat tasks.

In this chapter, you will learn how to define a question and find its corresponding answer. Additionally, you will learn how to configure Rasa to automatically identify a query (by finding a question that is semantically closest to the query) and give the corresponding answer. Finally, you will develop a practical understanding of these concepts with the help of the hands-on exercise provided at the end of the chapter.

In particular, in this chapter, we will cover the following topics:

- Defining retrieval intents – the questions users want to ask
- Defining responses – the answers to the questions
- Updating the configuration to use `ResponseSelector`
- Learning by doing – building an FAQ bot

Let's start by defining the user's problems.

Technical requirements

You can find all of the code-related files for this chapter in a directory named `ch05` at the following GitHub repository: `https://github.com/PacktPublishing/Conversational-AI-with-RASA`.

Defining retrieval intents – the questions users want to ask

First, we need to define the question and its corresponding intent. Note that the intent name for the training data of `ResponseSelector` is different from the ordinary intent names that we have discussed in *Chapter 2, Natural Language Understanding in Rasa*. `ResponseSelector` needs to follow the `<group>/<intent>` format in order to name the intents. This also explains why even ordinary intents should not have / as part of their name.

Here is an example:

```
nlu:
  - intent: chitchat/ask_name
    examples: |
       - What is your name?
     - Who are you?
     - How can I call you?
  - intent: chitchat/ask_weather
    examples: |
       - What's the weather like on your side?
     - It's sunny and clear here on my side, what about you?
```

You can see that the training data for `ResponseSelector` is in the same format as the intent training data except for the intent names. The `<group>` part of the `<group>/<intent>` format is called a retrieval intent in Rasa. Here, the two intents, `chitchat/ask_name` and `chtchat/ask_weather`, both belong to the `chitchat` retrieval intent.

Now that we have a clear idea of how to define the questions, we need to understand how to answer them. In the next section, we will discuss this in more depth.

Defining responses – the answers to the questions

First, we put the data of the answers inside the `responses` field in `domain.yml`.

Here is an example:

```
responses:
  utter_chitchat/ask_name
    - text: My name is Sarah, a Rasa documentation bot.
  utter_chitchat/ask_weather
    - text: My place is always sunny and clear.
```

In Rasa, every intent with the name of `<intent_name>` has a response called `utter_<intent_name>` as the answer. In this way, there is a connection between the question and the answer. Although in this example, we use plain text responses, you can respond with richer formats. Because these answers are defined using Rasa's responses, you can use any features supported by the responses (including but not limited to pictures as a reply, a channel-specific reply, or custom reply content).

Now that the question and the corresponding answer are ready, in the next section, we will discuss how to configure Rasa to match the user's question in general and how to correctly reply to the user with the relevant answer.

Updating the configuration to use ResponseSelector

In order to perform an intelligent categorization of the questions, we need to use the `ResponseSelector` NLU component to train a model with existing training data. We need to add the `ResponseSelector` component to the pipeline. The `ResponseSelector` component depends on the featurizer and intent classifier, so make sure you place it after these components in your pipeline, as follows:

```
pipeline:
  - name: XXXFeaturizer # replace this with a real Featurizer
  - name: XXXClassifier # replace this with a real Classifier
  - name: ResponseSelector
```

In order to get the right answer based on the result from `ResponseSelector`, we need to initiate `RulePolicy` and implement a rule to do the mapping. Here is an example:

```
rules:
  - rule: map to chitchat
    steps:
      - intent: chitchat
      - action: utter_chitchat
```

Here, we create a rule mapping between the `chitchat` retrieval intent and the `utter_chitchat` action (which is a template). When the dialogue system is running, `RulePolicy` will automatically trigger the `utter_chitchat` action when it encounters the `chitchat` intent.

At this point, we have discussed all of the theoretical parts. To check your understanding, we have prepared a special hands-on project for you in the next section.

Learning by doing – building an FAQ bot

In this section, the practical example has been designed to develop your practical understanding with regard to the concepts covered in the preceding sections.

We will create an FAQ bot based on a homemade toy-level dataset. This FAQ bot will answer questions for fresh graduates about participating in an interview at The Acme Corporation (a fictitious company from `https://en.wikipedia.org/wiki/Acme_Corporation`).

What are the features of our bot?

In this section, we will list all the functions this exercise project should provide. Let's start with the greeting and goodbye messages.

Handling greetings and goodbyes

Example #1: The bot responds to the user's greetings and provides a description of its own functions:

```
User: Hello!
Bot: Hello, I am Silly. I am a Rasa-based FAQ bot. I can help
you with answering questions about the recruitment of fresh
graduates for The Silly Company.
```

Example #2: The bot echoes goodbye to the user:

```
User: Bye bye!
Bot: Goodbye!
```

Handling FAQs about interviews

The bot can answer many questions. Here, I will introduce you to some of them.

Example #1: Answer questions about interview preparation:

```
User: What documents do I need to bring to the interview?
Bot: During the interview, please bring a valid certificate
that can prove your identity. For positions with special
requirements, please bring the original and copy of the
certificate that can prove your professionalism.
```

Example #2: Answer questions about how to obtain interview results:

```
User: How to check the interview result?
Bot: We will notify you of the result of the interview by email
or phone.
```

Although these features seem to be many, the implementation is not as complicated as you might think. In the next section, we will take you into the inside of this bot to examine how it is implemented.

How can we implement it?

Let's follow the official Rasa project structure:

```
.
├── config.yml
├── credentials.yml
├── data
│   ├── stories.yml
│   ├── rules.yml
│   └── nlu.yml
├── domain.yml
├── endpoints.yml
└── models
```

All the Rasa commands expect the proceeding project layout. With this layout, you can run most commands (such as `rasa train`, `rasa shell`, and `rasa test`) without any additional configuration.

Let's start with the train data.

Creating the NLU training data

In our project, all of the training questions are stored in the `data/nlu.yml` file. In this file, we have training data for two intents: `greet` and `goodbye`. To handle FAQs, we also need a retrieval intent: `faq`. We will create sub-intents for each question under the `faq` retrieval intent.

A part of the training data content (the full content has already been provided to you in the GitHub repository) is as follows:

```
version: "2.0"
nlu:
<-- greet and goodbye intents are omitted here. -->
  - intent: faq/interview_paperwork
    examples: |
      - What documents do I need to bring to the interview?
  - intent: faq/interview_result
    examples: |
      - How to check the interview result?
<-- we have omitted another sub-intents here. -->
```

Our question samples are now in place. Next, we will define the answers to those questions in the domain.

Creating the story data

Stories are stored in data/stories.yml file. The stories in this project are simple, that is, the greet intent will trigger the utter_greet action, and the goodbye intent will trigger the utter_goodbye action. The corresponding stories are as follows:

```
version: "2.0"
stories:
  - story: greet
    steps:
      - intent: greet
      - action: utter_greet
  - story: say goodbye
    steps:
      - intent: goodbye
      - action: utter_goodbye
```

Next, we will discuss the rules that you need to follow when mapping retrieval intents to responses.

Creating rules for the response users' questions

Rules are stored in the data/rules.yml file. In this project, we only have one rule, that is, to map a retrieval intent to a response. The corresponding rule is as follows:

```
rules:
  - rule: respond to FAQs
    steps:
      - intent: faq
      - action: utter_faq
```

Next, we will define the answers to those questions in the domain.

Configuring the domain

Domain settings are stored in the domain.yml file. In this chapter, the settings are essentially the same as those that were introduced in previous chapters. The slight difference is that this chapter adds some answers to the responses field, which correspond to the questions introduced in the *Creating NLU training data* section. The outline of the domain file is as follows:

```yaml
version: "2.0"
intents:
  - goodbye
  - greet
  - faq
responses:
  utter_greet:
    - text: Hello, I am Silly. I am a Rasa-based FAQ bot. I
can help you with answering questions about the recruitment of
fresh graduates for The Silly Company.
  utter_goodbye:
- text: Goodbye!
  utter_faq/interview_paperwork:
    - text: During the interview, please bring a valid
certificate that can prove your identity. For positions with
special requirements, please bring the original and copy of the
certificate that can prove your professionalism.
  utter_faq/interview_result:
- text: We will notify you of the result of the interview by
email or phone.
    <-- we have omitted some responses here. -->
actions:
  - utter_goodbye
  - utter_greet
  - utter_default
  - utter_faq
```

In this domain, the responses with the utter_faq/interview_paperwork key and the utter_faq/interview_result key answer the corresponding questions (faq/interview_paperwork and faq/interview_result).

In the next step, we will configure Rasa so that it can perform the functions we want.

Configuring the pipelines and policies

The configurations of the pipelines and policies are stored in the config.yml file. In the pipeline part, we need to ensure that the ResponseSelector component is included. In the policies field, we need to make sure that the RulePolicy is included. The complete content of the config.yml file is as follows:

```
language: en

pipeline:
  - name: WhitespaceTokenizer
  - name: LanguageModelFeaturizer
    model_name: bert
    model_weights: "rasa/LaBSE"
  - name: "DIETClassifier"
    epochs: 100
    learning_rate: 0.001
  - name: ResponseSelector

policies:
  - name: MemoizationPolicy
  - name: TEDPolicy
  - name: RulePolicy
```

The pipeline part is the classical NLU pipeline for English (with BERT as the core model). The policies part uses a combination of TEDPolicy, MemoizationPolicy, and RulePolicy, which have already proved to be useful for dialogue management.

At this point, all the data and configurations are ready. In the next step, we will start training the model.

Training models

We will use the command-line tool that comes with Rasa for model training. The specific steps are as follows. Open a command-line Terminal in the project directory and enter the following command:

```
rasa train
```

After waiting for the completion of the command, the training of the model is over. The newly generated model file will be located in the `models` directory under the project directory.

In the next section, we will use Rasa's own tools to start the service and make inferences.

Running the Rasa server and using a client to make inferences

In order to reduce the complexity of the deployment, in this project, we will use Rasa's built-in `rasa shell` command as the client.

When `rasa shell` starts, it will also start the Rasa server in the background. Therefore, there is no need to start the Rasa server independently. Additionally, since custom actions are not used in this project, there is no need to start the Rasa action server.

In order to run the Rasa shell instance, open the Terminal application in the project directory and type in the following command:

```
rasa shell
```

Once the model has been loaded by `rasa shell`, we can interact with the bot in the shell command line:

```
Your input -> How to check the interview result?
We will notify you of the result of the interview by email or phone.
```

Congratulations! You have successfully made an FAQ bot. Now you should have a deeper understanding of how to define questions and answers and how to configure Rasa to choose an appropriate answer to the user's question.

Summary

In this chapter, you learned to use `ResponseSelector` to handle chitchat and FAQs. This usually requires three steps. First, you need to define retrieval intents, given enough samples about the questions that users might ask. Note that the retrieval intents are slightly different from ordinary intents (if you do not remember the differences, please try to review this chapter). Second, you need to define your responses, that is, the answers to the questions. Remember that there is a rule about how to pair the answers with the questions. Third, you need to update the configuration (both in the `pipeline` field and the `polices` field) to use `ResponseSelector` and `RulePolicy` to make the bot work correctly.

In the next chapter, we will examine how to use knowledge base actions to handle knowledge base question answering.

6
Knowledge Base Actions to Handle Question Answering

In the previous chapter, we introduced, in detail, the process of using `ResponseSelector` to handle chitchat and FAQs. This chapter will teach you how to deal with more complex question answering problems: referential resolution and dynamic query. Referential resolution refers to correctly parsing the pronouns (such as *it*, *the first*, and *the last*) into corresponding concrete objects. The dynamic query problem means that the query result might change rapidly. It might be different each time, so it is impossible to use fixed reply content, as we did in the previous chapter.

In this chapter, you will learn how to create a knowledge base that can be used for answering questions. Additionally, you will learn to customize knowledge base actions, learn how referential resolution (mapping a mention to an object) works, and how to create a knowledge base. Finally, you will develop a practical understanding of these concepts with the help of the hands-on exercise provided at the end of this chapter.

In particular, in this chapter, we will cover the following topics:

- Why we need knowledge base actions – understanding the problems we want to solve
- How to use knowledge base actions
- How to customize knowledge base actions
- Learning by doing – building a knowledge-based music query chatbot

Let's begin by gaining an understanding of the problems we want to solve.

Technical requirements

You can find all the files for this chapter inside the `ch06` directory of the GitHub repository at `https://github.com/PacktPublishing/Conversational-AI-with-RASA`.

> **A knowledge base action is an experimental feature**
>
> At the time of writing (Rasa version 2.5), the knowledge base action that we are discussing here is still an experimental feature. The functionality might be changed, or (although unlikely, it is still possible) it can be removed in the future.

Why do we need knowledge base actions?

One of the common challenges you face when building a chatbot is that users might not refer to things using names but with pronouns such as "it," "this," and "that" or "the previous one" and "the second one." Here is an example:

```
User:
    Do you have any recommended songs for me?
Bot:
    I find the following songs:
    1: Billie Jean
    2: The Shape of My Heart
    3: Like a Rolling Stone
User:
    Which album is the first song?
Bot:
    "Billie Jean" is from Michael Jackson's album "Thriller".
```

In the preceding example, `User` refers to `Billie Jean` as the `first song`. This pattern is common in spoken language, especially when the name of the item is uncommon (for example, IKEA's "FRAKATA Carrier Bag") or the name is too long (for example, IKEA's "MACKAPÄR Bench with storage compartments white 100x51 cm"). In order to be able to correctly handle this kind of dialogue that uses referents to represent objects, the dialogue management system needs to remember the messages that were previously sent to the user (in this case, it is the song list) in order to correctly extract the corresponding objects from these pronouns.

In real-life scenarios, users will also ask about the object's properties, such as the album name of a song or the average cost per person at a restaurant. A knowledge base on music and restaurants is necessary to answer these kinds of questions from the user. However, in some domains, this information is dynamic and keeps changing all the time, for example, the price of hotels or plane tickets. Therefore, all of this information cannot be hardcoded.

In the next section, we will introduce a knowledge base action, which is a specially designed feature to handle those problems.

How do you use knowledge base actions?

To tackle the challenges that we introduced in the previous section, Rasa can be integrated with a knowledge base via a knowledge base action. A knowledge base action is a special action that has been developed to handle referential resolution and queries on objects and their properties.

In general, to use knowledge base actions, you need to do the following:

- Create a knowledge base from where the bot can retrieve information that will be used to answer the questions that have been asked.

- Create a knowledge base action using Rasa SDK, which will query the knowledge base according to the user's inputs and reply with relevant answers.

- Define some **Natural Language Understanding** (NLU) data so that users can trigger the knowledge base action via the inputs.

- Modify your knowledge base actions to make the responses more human-like.

Let's start by defining a knowledge base.

Creating a knowledge base

A knowledge base stores the data that is used to answer a user's questions. It can be used to store data with many complicated structures (for instance, a knowledge base about movies could include the directors, actors, showtime, awards won, film companies, box office revenue, and more). Here, we will use the built-in InMemoryKnowledgeBase. As the name implies, InMemoryKnowledgeBase is a simple knowledge base storage class that puts all data into memory. Although this will make it impossible for you to store knowledge base data that exceeds the memory size, and means that you cannot store complicated data structures, it is recommended that you use it for smaller applications because it is simple to use and does not require any third-party library support. For large-scale applications, thanks to the powerful extensibility of Rasa, you can create and use your own custom knowledge base. We will explain how to do this, in detail, in the *Learning by doing – building a knowledge-based music query chatbot* section of this chapter.

To use InMemoryKnowledgeBase, developers need to provide knowledge base data in a JSON file. The following example contains data on songs and singers. Every type of object in the knowledge base should have a key. For example, here, the keys are song and singer. Additionally, every type of object needs to be mapped to a list of objects, as shown in the following example:

```
{
    "song": [
        {
            "id": 0,
            "name": "Billie Jean",
            "singer": "Michael Jackson",
            "album": "Thriller",
            "style": "Rock"
        },
        <-- we have omitted some similar items here. -->
    ],
    "singer": [
        {
            "id": 0,
            "name": "Bob Dylan",
            "gender": "male",
            "birthday": "1941/05/24"
        },
        <-- we have omitted some similar items here. -->
```

```
    ]
}
```

In the default implementation of `InMemoryKnowledgeBase`, just as in the preceding example, every object should, at the very least, have `name` and `id` properties.

With the data file (named `data.json`), developers can create an instance of `InMemoryKnowledgeBase`. This knowledge instance will pass to a knowledge base action as an argument.

In the next section, we will learn how to create a knowledge base action.

Creating a custom knowledge base action

Developers can create their own custom knowledge base action by inheriting the `ActionQueryKnowledgeBase` class and then transferring the knowledge base instance as a parameter to the `constructor` function. This is shown in the following example:

```
from rasa_sdk.knowledge_base.storage import
InMemoryKnowledgeBase
from rasa_sdk.knowledge_base.actions import
ActionQueryKnowledgeBase
class MyKnowledgeBaseAction(ActionQueryKnowledgeBase):
    def name(self) -> Text:
        return "action_response_query"

    def __init__(self):
        knowledge_base = InMemoryKnowledgeBase("data.json")
        super().__init__(knowledge_base)
```

Here, we use the `data.json` file as the data source to create an instance of `InMemoryKnowledgeBase`, and then transfer it as the knowledge base instance to the constructor function of `ActionQueryKnowledgeBase`.

Now, we can put our own action into the domain configuration:

```
actions:
  - action_response_query
```

Now we have a knowledge base and a knowledge base action. The final piece of the puzzle is to define some NLU data and stories to allow users to perform a knowledge base action via their input. We will cover this topic in the next section.

Defining NLU data and stories to perform queries from users

In order to let the chatbot know that the user wants to do a knowledge base query, developers need to define an intent to express this. Here, we define the intent as `query_knowledge_base`.

Note that `ActionQueryKnowledgeBase` is able to handle two types of requests from users:

- Users who want to get the list of a specific object type, with or without any filtering conditions

- Users who want to get a specific attribute of an object

Both types of requests should be under the intent of `query_knowledge_base`. Here is an example of the NLU data:

```
version: "2.0"
nlu:
  - intent: query_knowledge_base
    examples: |
      - List me some [songs](object_type)
      - List me some [singers](object_type)
      - List me some [songs](object_type) of [Sting](singer)
      - [That song](mention) belongs to what [album](attribute)
      - [Album](attribute) of [First](mention)
      - [Album](attribute) of [Billie Jean](song)?
      - [Birthday](attribute) of [Lady Gaga](singer)
```

In the example NLU data, we have three different entity types. They are the key to performing a knowledge-based query:

- `object_type`: This gives the information type of what the user wants to query. For example, when a user says `List me some songs` the user wants to query songs. Therefore, we need to mark `songs` as an entity of `object_type`, so our bot knows about the user's interest in the query. Additionally, we need to convert `songs` into `song` by using synonym mapping. This is because our knowledge base has a key named `song` but not `songs`.

- `mention`: This gives indirect information about what the user wants to specify. In daily language expressions, we often use `this`, `the first`, `the last`, or similar words to refer to the object we are interested in. For example, when a user says `What album did the first one belong to?`, in this query, the user wants to query an attribute of a song, and this song is the first song of our song list that we showed to the user in the earlier conversational turns. We need to mark `the first one` as an entity of `mention`, so our bot can resolve this indirect information to the song.

- `attribute`: This specifies the information (or attribute) that the user wants to know about the object. For example, when a user says `What is the album of Billie Jean?`, no doubt, the user wants to know the `album` (that is, the attribute) of `Billie Jean` (that is, the object). In order for our bot to get such information (the attribute), we need to mark the `album` as an entity of `attribute`.

Remember to modify the `domain.yaml` file. Then, add the following configurations into the domain file:

```
entities:
  - object_type
  - mention
  - attribute

slots:
  object_type:
    type: any
  mention:
    type: any
  attribute:
    type: any
```

Finally, we need to add the corresponding story in `story.yml` to make sure the `action_query_knowledge_base` action can be executed when the user expresses the intent of `query_knowledge_base`. This is shown in the following example:

```
stories:
  - story: knowledge query
    steps:
      - intent: query_knowledge_base
      - action: action_response_query
```

We have now learned how to define NLU data and stories to trigger knowledge base actions. In the next section, we will explain how knowledge base actions work, that is, how a knowledge base action uses NLU data.

How do knowledge base actions work?

Interestingly, `ActionQueryKnowledgeBase` needs both the current extracted entity information and the slot from the previous conversations to understand the query target.

How do you query objects?

For query objects from the knowledge base, the user's request should contain the object type. Let's take a look at an example:

```
Do you have any recommended songs for me?
```

This question contains the target query object: songs. The NLU module should understand this sentence as `Do you have any recommended [songs](object_ type) for me`, and songs should be mapped to the `song` object type. The system will then be able to query the song knowledge base and list its entities.

If the user inputs something such as `Give me some songs from Michael Jackson`, then the user wants to have a song list from the object that has the singer attribute as `Michael Jackson`. NLU will understand this sentence as `Give me some [songs](object_type) from [Michael Jackson](singer)`. Here, the singer entity with the value of `Michael Jackson` gives the filter condition for the query.

How do you query the attributes of an object?

If a user wants to get some specific information about one particular object, the user's request should contain both the object information and the attribute of interest. For example, the user might input (after NLU processing) the following:

```
Which [album](attribute) does [Billie Jean](song) belong to?
```

Here, the user wants to query the `album` (attribute) of the `Billie Jean` (object) song. The system should extract the `song` type entity with the value of `Billie Jean` and the `attribute` type entity with the value of `album`. The entity of the `song` type is used to target the object, and the entity of the `attribute` type is used to target the attribute of that object.

How do you perform reference resolution?

In real-life situations, sometimes, users will not directly use the song name to refer to the object. They might use something like an ordinal number or a pronoun to refer to the object that already appears in the previous conversation (messages), as shown in the following example:

```
Bot:
    I find the following songs:
    1: Billie Jean
    2: The Shape of My Heart
    3: Like a Rolling Stone
User:
    Which album does the first one belong to?
```

It is the task of the action to be able to correctly map those references (in this example, this is the first one) to the object in the knowledge base. ActionQueryKowledgeBase can carry out two types of reference resolution:

- An ordinal number reference, for example, the first one

- A pronoun reference, for example, this one

Ordinal number references

An ordinal number reference means that an object is referred to by its position in the list. For example, take a look at the following:

```
User:
    Do you have any recommended songs for me?
Bot:
    I find the following songs:
    1: Billie Jean
    2: The Shape of My Heart
    3: Like a Rolling Stone
User:
    Which album is the first song?
```

Here, the user inputs the first song to refer to Billie Jean. Some other examples of ordinal number references include the second one, last one, and any. Normally, the user uses an ordinal number reference when the system outputs a list of results in the previous round of conversation. To resolute/map the ordinal numbers to a real object, we need to set up a mapping relationship in ActionQueryKnowledgeBase. The default settings (that is, the ordinal_mention_mapping attribute of the KnowledgeBase class) are as follows:

```
{
    "1": lambda l: l[0],
    "2": lambda l: l[1],
    "3": lambda l: l[2],
    "4": lambda l: l[3],
    "5": lambda l: l[4],
    "6": lambda l: l[5],
    "7": lambda l: l[6],
    "8": lambda l: l[7],
    "9": lambda l: l[8],
    "10": lambda l: l[9],
    "ANY": lambda l: random.choice(l),
    "LAST": lambda l: l[-1],
}
```

This ordinal number mapping dictionary maps the ordinal number in a string type to an object in the list. For example, the lambda l: l[0] lambda function maps the string of 1 to the object with an index of 0 in the list, which is the first object in the list.

We can see from the dictionary that the ordinal number mapping dictionary does not contain keys such as the first one. Developers need to define the entity value mapping to map the different formats of ordinal number references from user expressions to the standard format. For example, we need to map the first one to 1 and the last one to LAST. Developers can define the NLU entity synonym mapping to achieve this. For example, take a look at the following:

```
nlu:
  - synonym: '1'
    examples: |
      - The first one
      - First
      - Number one
```

Although the NLU module detects that `First` is a reference, it can still use the entity synonym mapping to map `First` to `1`. Then, `ActionQueryKnowledgeBase` can map `First` to the target object of `Billie Jean`.

Other references

When discussing a specific object, people often do not use the name of the object. Instead, they use pronouns such as "it", "that one," and more. Let's take a look at an example:

```
User:
    Do you have any recommended songs for me?
Bot:
    I find the following songs:
    1: Billie Jean
    2: The Shape of My Heart
    3: Like a Rolling Stone
User:
    Which album is the first song?
Bot:
    "Billie Jean" is from Michael Jackson's album "Thriller".
User:
    Which year was it published?
```

When a user says `Which year was it published`, here, `it` refers to `Billie Jean`. NLU detects that the value of `mention` is `it`; therefore, `ActionQueryKnowledgeBase` will map the `mention` entity to the object that was last mentioned: `Billie Jean`.

How do you customize knowledge base actions?

The default knowledge base action has several disadvantages. First, the message returned to the user is not very user-friendly, the reply format is fixed, and it does not have any personality. Second, the built-in memory-based knowledge base is limited by the size of the memory and cannot support a very large-scale knowledge base. Additionally, there is no way to modify the content of the knowledge base externally in real time. In the following sections, we will solve these problems one by one.

Modifying ActionQueryKnowledgeBase to customize the behavior

Here, we introduce how to customize the output message from `ActionQueryKnowledgeBase`. This is especially important for Rasa developers who use multiple languages, as the default return message is always English.

Custom ways to express the object list

When a user requests the bot system to return the list of objects, `utter_objects()` will be called. The function of `utter_objects()` is to return the object list to the user. Here is an example in default condition:

```
Found the following objects of type 'song': 1: Billie Jean 2:
The Shape of My Heart 3: Like a Rolling Stone
```

If no object is found, the default response will be like this:

```
I could not find any objects of type 'song'.
```

Usually, this kind of default response is not suitable for use in a commercial product. We must return the response content that best fits the context. This can be achieved by customizing `utter_objects()`.

Custom ways to express the attribute of an object

When a user requests the bot system to return a specific attribute of some object, `utter_attribute_value()` will be called. This function returns the query results to the user.

If the target attribute is found, the default response will be like this:

```
'Billie Jean' has the value 'Thriller' for attribute 'album'.
```

If the attribute is not found, the default response is as follows:

```
Did not find a valid value for attribute 'album' for object
'Billie Jean'
```

Of course, we also need to customize `utter_attribute_value()` to modify the response content here.

Customizing InMemoryKnowledgeBase

InMemoryKnowledgeBase inherits the KnowledgeBase class. We can overload the following functions to implement a custom InMemoryKnowledgeBase:

- get_key_attribute_of_object(): This changes the key attribute of the object in the knowledge base.

- get_representation_function_of_object(): This changes the way you can express the object to users.

- set_ordinal_mention_mapping(): This changes how you can map the mention to the object in the list.

First, let's take a look at how to get the key attribute of an object.

Changing the key attribute of an object

In order to track the last object that the user mentioned, we need to store a key attribute for the object. Each object should have a key attribute that is globally unique, just like the keys in a relational database. By default, the name of the key attribute is id. Developers can call set_key_attribute_of_object() to modify it.

Changing the way to show objects to users

First, let's figure out how the knowledge base action represents an object to the user. Then, we will figure out how to change it. Let's view an example restaurant, as follows:

```
{
    "id": 1,
    "name": "Italian World",
    "cuisine": "pizza",
    "private_room": false,
    "price-range": "cheap"
}
```

When a user requests the bot system to output all the restaurants, we do not necessarily need to output all the details of the restaurants. Developers should give a simple, meaningful, and unique representation. In fact, in most circumstances, the representation will be the name of the object.

Here, `get_representation_function_of_object()` returns a function that maps the object to its representation. By default, the value of the representation is `lambda obj: obj["name"]`, which is the object name. When there is no name attribute for the object, or there is ambiguity in the name attribute, developers should call `set_representation_fuction_of_object()` to modify it.

Changing the mapping from a mention to an object

Ordinal mention mapping is used to map an ordinal number reference, for example, *the second one*, to an object in the list. By default, ordinal mention mapping is defined as follows (this can be found in the `set_ordinal_mention_mapping()` method of the `ActionQueryKowledgeBase` class):

```
{
    "1": lambda l: l[0],
    "2": lambda l: l[1],
    "3": lambda l: l[2],
    "4": lambda l: l[3],
    "5": lambda l: l[4],
    "6": lambda l: l[5],
    "7": lambda l: l[6],
    "8": lambda l: l[7],
    "9": lambda l: l[8],
    "10": lambda l: l[9],
    "ANY": lambda l: random.choice(l),
    "LAST": lambda l: l[-1],
}
```

Developers can set the mapping relationship by calling the `set_ordinal_mention_mapping()` function of the knowledge base class (using the mapping dictionary as input). Under normal circumstances, the default settings are able to cover most occasions. Unless you know what you are doing, it is not recommended that you modify the mapping relationship.

Building your own knowledge base

When the volume of data is too large or the data structure is too complicated, developers may need to create a custom knowledge base. This is done by inheriting `KnowledgeBase` and implementing the `get_objects()`, `get_object()` and `get_attributes_of_object()` methods.

The `get_objects()` method is used to query the knowledge base for objects of the given type (for example, the `object_type` entity/slot), and filter the objects by the `attributes` (that is, the `attribute` entity/slot) if any attributes are given.

The `get_object()` method is used to return the object of the given type (the `object_type` entity/slot) that matches the given object identifier, that is, the key attribute or the string representation of the object (by default, this is the `name` field of the object).

The `get_attributes_of_object()` method is used to return a list of all of the attributes that belong to the provided object type.

In the next section, we will use what we have learned so far to carry out some exercises. We will define a new knowledge base on our own.

Learning by doing – building a knowledge-based music query chatbot

We have designed this section to enhance your understanding of knowledge base actions. We will create a QA bot based on a homemade toy-level knowledge base. This QA robot will answer questions regarding music: songs, albums, and singers.

What are the features of our bot?

In this section, we will introduce the characteristics of our robot. Its features can be divided into two types: one is the unconstrained query, and the other is the constrained query (or with filter conditions). The former does not make any constraints or filters on the query object, such as *list all singers*. The latter has clear constraints, such as *List all-male singers born in 1980*, where *born in 1980* and *male* are both constraints.

To begin, let's discuss the unconstrained query.

Querying the list of objects and asking for the attributes of the specified object

Example #1: Search for songs and ask for the album attributes of the specified song (via mention):

```
User:
    List me some songs
Bot:
    Find the following songs:
```

```
1: Billie Jean

2: Like a Rolling Stone

3: The Shape of My Heart
User:
What is the first album?
Bot:
The album of Billie Jean is Thriller.
```

Example #2: Query the singer and ask for the birthday attribute of the specified singer (by name):

```
User:
List me some singers
Bot:
Find the following singers:

1: Bob Dylan

2: Michael Jackson

3: Lady Gaga

4: Sting
User:
The birthday of Michael Jackson
Bot:
The birthday of Michael Jackson is 1958/08/29.
```

In this section, we illustrated that our robot can return a list of objects and the attributes of a given object. In the next section, we will demonstrate that our robot can return a list of objects with constraints.

Querying a list of objects that meet specific attribute requirements

Example #1: Query the list of songs and request that the singer attribute (that is, the singer) of the song is Jay Chou:

```
User:
List me some songs of Lady Gaga
Bot:
Find the following songs:

1: Poker Face
```

Example #2: Query the list of singers and add a requirement that the singer's gender attribute is male:

```
User:
    List some male singers
Bot:
    Find the following singers:
    1: Bob Dylan
    2: Michael Jackson
    3: Sting
```

How do we implement the bot?

Let's follow the official Rasa project structure:

```
├── actions
│   └── actions.py
├── config.yml
├── credentials.yml
├── data
│   ├── stories.yml
│   └── nlu.yml
├── domain.yml
├── endpoints.yml
├── neo4j_knowledge_base.py
└── models
```

In this chapter, the project directory is almost the same as the official standard directory layout of Rasa. The only difference is that there is an extra file in the directory of this chapter: neo4j_knowledge_base.py. This file is used to implement a Neo4j-based knowledge base, which we will discuss later.

To understand how to implement our robot, let's start with the training data.

Creating the NLU training data

In our project, all of the training NLU data is stored in the `data/nlu.yml` file. In this file, we need some training data for intent: `query_knowledge_base`. We will use this intent to express that users want to query something in the knowledge base.

Part of the training data content (the full content has already been provided to you in the GitHub repository) is as follows:

```
version: "2.0"
nlu:
  - intent: query_knowledge_base
    examples: |
      - List me some [songs](object_type)
      - List me some [singers](object_type)
      - List me some [songs](object_type) of [Sting](singer)
      - List me [songs](object_type) of [Bob Dylan](singer)
      - List [songs](object_type) of [Lady Gaga](singer)
      - List me [songs](object_type) of [Lady Gaga](singer)
      - [That song](mention) belongs to what [album](attribute)
      - Who is the [singer](attribute) of [the previous song](mention)
      - [Album](attribute) of [First](mention)
      - [Album](attribute) of [Billie Jean](song)?
      - [The Shape of My Heart](song) belongs to what [album](attribute)?
      - [Poker Face](song) is in what [album](attribute)?
      - [Birthday](attribute) of [First](mention)
      - [Birthday](attribute) of [Lady Gaga](singer)
```

In the preceding NLU training data, we have created some training examples to represent the questions that users might ask our bot.

The next step is to create story data to make sure that the `query_knowledge_base` intent can always trigger the execution of the knowledge base action.

Creating the story data

Stories are stored in the `data/stories.yml` file. Stories in this project are simple, that is, the `query_knowledge_base` intent will trigger the `action_response_query` action, which is the knowledge base action that will be defined later in this chapter. The corresponding stories are as follows:

```
version: "2.0"
stories:
   <-- we have omitted some stories for greet and goodbye here.
 -->
  - story: knowledge query
    steps:
       - intent: query_knowledge_base
       - action: action_response_query
```

Next, we will learn about the configuration of the domain.

Configuring the domain

Domain settings are stored in the `domain.yml` file. In this chapter, the settings are, essentially, the same as those that were introduced in previous chapters. We need to add all the slots and entities that are used by the knowledge base actions. An outline of the domain file is as follows:

```
intents:
  - goodbye
  - greet
  - query_knowledge_base:
      use_entities: [ ]
entities:
  - object_type
  - mention
  - attribute
  - object-type
  - song
  - singer
  - gender
slots:
```

```
    attribute:
      type: any
    gender:
      type: any
    mention:
      type: any
    object_type:
      type: any
    singer:
      type: any
    song:
      type: any
  responses:
  <-- we have omitted all the responses here. -->
  actions:
    - action_response_query
  <-- we have omitted other actions here. -->
```

If the name of your knowledge base action is not `action_query_knowledge_base`, which is the default one, then you need to add the following content to the slots field of the domain:

```
    knowledge_base_last_object:
      type: any
    knowledge_base_last_object_type:
      type: any
    knowledge_base_listed_objects:
      type: any
    knowledge_base_objects:
      type: any
```

Our customized knowledge base action will use those slots. If those slots are not defined, our knowledge base action will not work correctly.

In the next step, we will configure the pipelines and policies for Rasa.

Configuring the pipelines and polices

The configurations of the pipelines and policies are stored in the `config.yml` file. In this project, the pipeline settings and policy configurations are nothing special. Here, we use the configuration that we already introduced and used in previous chapters. Our full configuration (that is, the content of `config.yml`) is shown as follows:

```yaml
language: en
pipeline:
  - name: WhitespaceTokenizer
  - name: LanguageModelFeaturizer
    model_name: bert
    model_weights: "rasa/LaBSE"
  - name: "DIETClassifier"
    epochs: 100
    learning_rate: 0.001
policies:
  - name: MemoizationPolicy
  - name: TEDPolicy
  - name: RulePolicy
```

At this point, all of the normal setting parts of Rasa are complete. In the next section, we will discuss everything to do with the knowledge base. Let's start with knowledge base data.

Creating our knowledge base data

As discussed earlier (in the *Creating a knowledge base* subsection of the *How do you use knowledge base actions?* section), the built-in knowledge base data is stored in a JSON file. For this project, we created a homemade toy-level knowledge base, and we stored it in a JSON file, as shown in the following code block:

```json
{
  "song": [
    {
      "id": 0,
      "name": "Billie Jean",
      "singer": "Michael Jackson",
      "album": "Thriller",
      "style": "Rock"
```

```
    },
    <-- we have omitted some items here. -->
    {
      "id": 3,
      "name": "Poker Face",
      "singer": "Lady Gaga",
      "album": "The Fame",
      "style": "dance-pop"
    }
  ],
  "singer": [
    {
      "id": 0,
      "name": "Bob Dylan",
      "gender": "male",
      "birthday": "1941/05/24"
    },
    <-- we have omitted some items here. -->
    {
      "id": 3,
      "name": "Sting",
      "gender": "male",
      "birthday": "1951/10/02"
    }
  ]
}
```

In this JSON file, we define two types of objects: song and singer. Then, we add some instances (such as a dictionary of attributes) for each type.

The knowledge base data will be used by knowledge base action. In the next section, we will give a detailed introduction to knowledge base actions.

Creating our first knowledge base action

In general, using Rasa SDK to create a vanilla knowledge base action is pretty easy. What we need to do is create our own knowledge base action to inherit the `ActionQueryKnowledgeBase` base class and override the `name` method and the `__init__` method to inject our own knowledge base data. The code is as follows:

```python
from rasa_sdk.knowledge_base.actions import
ActionQueryKnowledgeBase
from rasa_sdk.knowledge_base.storage import
InMemoryKnowledgeBase


class MyKnowledgeBaseAction(ActionQueryKnowledgeBase):
    def name(self) -> Text:
        return "action_response_query"

    def __init__(self):
        knowledge_base = InMemoryKnowledgeBase("data.json")

        super().__init__(knowledge_base)
```

In the `__init__` method, first, we created an instance of `InMemoryKnowledgeBase` using our own knowledge base stored in the `data.json` file. Then, we passed this knowledge base object to the `__init__` method of `ActionQueryKnowledgeBase`.

Unfortunately, the current response that has been generated from this action is not user-friendly. We need to carry out more work to customize this knowledge base action. We will discuss this topic in more detail in the next section.

Customizing our knowledge base action

There are two methods we need to override to produce a more user-friendly response.

The first one is `utter_objects()`. This method is used to send a list of found objects (usually in the form of text) to the user to inform the user of the result of the query. In our project, we will override this method using the following code:

```
async def utter_objects(
    self,
    dispatcher,
    object_type,
    objects,
) -> None:
    if objects:
        dispatcher.utter_message(text=f"Found the following
{object_type}s:")

        repr_function = await utils.call_potential_
coroutine(
            self.knowledge_base.get_representation_
function_of_object(object_type)
        )

        for I, obj in enumerate(objects, 1):
            dispatcher.utter_message(text=""{i}: {repr_
function(obj)"")
    else:
        dispatcher.utter_message(text=""I did''t find any
{object_type}s"")
```

The second one is `utter_attribute_value()`. This method is used to send out a response, which tells the user the value of the attribute of interest. In our project, we will override this method using the following code:

```
def utter_attribute_value(
    self,
    dispatcher,
    object_name,
    attribute_name,
    attribute_value,
) -> None:
```

```
        if attribute_value:
            dispatcher.utter_message(
                text=f"{object_name}'s {attribute_name} is
{attribute_value}."
            )
        else:
            dispatcher.utter_message(
                text=f"I didn't
    find {object_name}'s {attribute_name}."
            )
```

In this code, if we get the `attribute_value` (that is, it is not `None`), we send a message to the user of the value of the attribute. If we do not get the `attribute_value` (that is, it is a `None`), we send a message to the user that the bot could not find the attribute.

Training a model, starting the server, and making inferences

We are using a standard directory layout, so we can use the default command to train the model. Typing this into your Terminal (or Command Prompt for Windows):

```
rasa train
```

After executing the preceding command, we have completed the training of the model. We will have our model in the `models` directory.

Now it is time to run it. There are two servers that we need to start up: the Rasa action server and the Rasa server.

We need to run the following command to run the Rasa action server:

```
rasa run actions
```

Since it is a server, it will keep running. To run another command, we need to open a new Terminal. In this new Terminal, we will run `rasa shell`, which we already mentioned in previous chapters. Here, `rasa shell` is a convenient tool; it not only runs the Rasa server in the background, but it also provides a Terminal-based interactive UI for the user to make inferences. Running `rasa shell` is easy. Just type the following command into your Terminal:

```
rasa shell
```

After the preceding command has been executed, we can interact with the bot in the shell command line by typing the input directly into the Terminal, as follows:

```
Your input -> List me some songs of Sting
    Find the following songs:
    1: The Shape of My Heart
```

Supporting the Neo4j knowledge base

Earlier (in the *Creating a knowledge base* subsection of the *How do you use knowledge base actions?* section), we introduced `InMemoryKnowledgeBase`, which is very easy to use and suitable for small applications. However, because it stores all of the data in memory, it cannot be used in large applications. The knowledge base of large applications is usually very large, complicated, and cannot be fully loaded into memory. Such large knowledge bases are usually managed by professional knowledge base software, such as `Neo4j`. `Neo4j` (`https://neo4j.com/`) is a graph database that is extremely popular in the industry; it has rich features. So, can we use the knowledge base based on `Neo4j` in Rasa? Of course, we can! We will discuss this in this section.

Before discussing the specific implementation any further, we have a decision regarding the code: we will not discuss the code of `Neo4j`. The code of `Neo4j` is beyond the scope of this book. Therefore, we will not explain how to use `Neo4j` (and its related code) in this chapter. You can learn about `Neo4j` through the official documentation (`https://neo4j.com/docs/`) or related books (`https://www.packtpub.com/catalogsearch/result/?q=Neo4j`). If you are interested in how we operate Neo4j, our GitHub project (`https://github.com/PacktPublishing/Conversational-AI-with-RASA/blob/main/Chapter06/neo4j_knowledge_base.py`) contains the complete `Neo4j` code for you to read.

Earlier (in the *Building your own knowledge base* subsection of the *How do you customize knowledge base actions?* section), we discussed how to create a new knowledge base instead of using `InMemoryKnowledgeBase`. You need to inherit `KnowledgeBase` and implement the `get_objects()`, `get_object()`, and `get_attributes_of_object()` methods.

Let's discuss the `get_objects()` first.

Overriding get_objects() to query the objects list from Neo4j

The function of get_objects() is to query the object list in Neo4j. Before we explain our ideas, let's take a look at its main code. The following is the code for get_objects():

```python
async def get_objects(
        self, object_type, attributes, limit = 5
):
        # convert attributes to dict
        attrs = {}
        for a in attributes:
            attrs[a["name"]] = a["value"]

        # transformer for query
        object_type = object_type.capitalize()

        # split into attrs and relations
        attrs_filter = {}
        relations_filter = {}
        relation = self.relation_attributes[object_type]
        for k, v in attrs.items():
            if k in relation:
                relations_filter[relation[k]] = v
            else:
                attrs_filter[k] = v
        # query Neo4j database
        result = self.do_get_objects(object_type, attrs_filter,
relations_filter, limit)

        return result
```

In the code of get_objects(), we performed the following steps:

1. First, we normalized object_type to make it completely consistent with the node type in Neo4j.

2. Next, we divided the attribute filtering into node attributes and relational queries according to our data structure in Neo4j.

3. Finally, we used `Neo4j` (by calling `self.do_get_objects()`) to perform such a query.

The next function that we need to implement is `get_object()`.

Overriding get_object() to query an object from Neo4j

The `get_object()` function returns the corresponding object by querying the object identifier (which is the input parameter of the function) in the `Neo4j` database. This logic is not hard. First, we normalize the query input. Second, we send the query to a helper function, named `self.do_get_object()`, which will access the `Neo4j` database and fetch the results. The code is as follows:

```
async def get_object(
    self, object_type, object_identifier
):
    # transformer for query
    object_type = object_type.capitalize()

    # query Neo4j
    result = self.do_get_object(
        object_type,
        object_identifier,
        await self.get_key_attribute_of_object(object_
type),
        await self.get_representation_attribute_of_
object(object_type),
    )

    return result
```

In the next section, we will examine how to override `get_attributes_of_object()`.

Overriding get_attributes_of_object() to get the attributes of an object type

The last piece we need to implement is the `get_attributes_of_object()` method. It returns a list of all the attributes that belong to the provided object type. Our implementation for this method is as follows:

```
async def get_attributes_of_object(self, object_type):
    # transformer for query
    object_type = object_type.capitalize()
    # get attribute from Neo4j
    result = self.do_get_attributes_of_object(object_type)
    return result
```

Congratulations! You have successfully made a knowledge-based music query chatbot. Now, you should have a deeper understanding of how to create a knowledge base action and how to configure NLU and dialogue management to trigger knowledge base actions following a user's request. You also learned how to use `Neo4j` as your knowledge base in a knowledge base action.

Summary

In this chapter, we introduced how to use knowledge base actions to handle question answering. First, you learned how to create an in-memory knowledge base for retrieving information that can be used to answer questions. Second, you were introduced to the working principles of knowledge base actions and learned how to configure NLU and dialogue management systems so that user requests can trigger knowledge base actions. Third, you learned how to modify knowledge base actions to customize them to your business and how to create a knowledge base by using your own code. Finally, we also built a knowledge-based music query chatbot, step by step, to help you understand those concepts better.

In the next chapter, we will discuss entity roles and groups for complex **Named Entity Recognition** (**NER**).

7
Entity Roles and Groups for Complex Named Entity Recognition

In *Chapter 2, Natural Language Understanding in Rasa*, we introduced how to carry out **Named Entity Recognition (NER)** in Rasa. NER extracts the entity type and the entity value from a piece of text. Unfortunately, for complex NER, we require more information than simply the entity type and the entity value. In this chapter, we will introduce the entity roles and entity groups for dealing with complex NER problems. The entity role can be used to distinguish the different semantic roles of entities (that have the same entity type). In comparison, the entity group can be used to group entities into different groups, where each grouped entity belongs to different subtasks in the same request.

In this chapter, you will learn how entity roles and entity groups can be used to solve the complex NER problem. Additionally, you will learn how to define training data, configure pipelines, and write stories for entity roles and entity groups. Finally, you will develop a practical understanding with the help of the hands-on exercise provided at the end of this chapter.

In this chapter, in particular, we will cover the following topics:

- Why do we need entity roles and entity groups?
- Using entity roles to distinguish semantics roles in entities of the same type
- Using entity groups to divide entities into groups
- Configuring Rasa to use entity roles and groups
- Learning by doing – building a ticket and drink booking bot

Let's begin by discussing why we need entity roles and entity groups.

Technical requirements

You can find all of the files for this chapter inside the directory named `ch07` in the following GitHub repository: `https://github.com/PacktPublishing/Conversational-AI-with-RASA`.

Why do we need entity roles and entity groups?

Sometimes, it is not enough to only have the entity type and entity value to accomplish a complicated task. We need to distinguish entities at a more granular level. Rasa provides two additional pieces of information about an entity: its role and group.

You can use entity roles to distinguish entities from the same entity type. For example, in your bot system, you can use an entity of the city type to mark a traveler's departure and arrival cities. Since both the departure and the destination are marked as city types, the bot cannot distinguish which one is the departure. In this case, you can use the entity role information to determine which city entity is the departure city and which one is the arrival city.

For more complex expressions, users could express two or more different requests at the same time. This time, understanding how to distinguish between which entities belong to the same group of requests will be critical to task execution. For example, consider a user who requests a glass of juice with ice and a glass of soda without ice. Because of the flexibility of user expression (for example, *a glass of juice with ice; a glass of soda without ice* and *a glass of juice and a glass of soda, the latter with ice, the former without ice*), there are many possibilities for the relative order of key entities (that is, juice, soda, with ice, and without ice). Therefore, the robot has no way of knowing which drink needs ice. In this case, using entity groups can help us to distinguish which entities are in a group. Each group represents a subtask, and the entities in the same group belong to the same subtask.

Using entity roles to distinguish semantics roles in entities of the same type

Rasa offers entity roles in which to distinguish the different roles of the same entity type. Let's take a look at an example of booking a flight ticket between New York and Chicago. If the system does not distinguish the departure and destination roles of the city entity, the bot will not able to understand whether the ticket is from New York to Chicago or from Chicago to New York. With the entity role, the entity has additional information that represents its semantic role (such as the departure or the destination), which will solve this problem for the bot.

To use entity roles, we need to annotate our training data with the role information along with the entity type. Some sample training data appears as follows:

```
A flight ticket from [New York]{"entity": "city",
"role": "departure"} to [Chicago]{"entity":"city",
"role":"destination"}
```

In the preceding sample data, we can note the following:

- We annotate New York as an entity of the city type and a role of departure. Then, we annotate Chicago as an entity of the city type and a role of destination.

- With the role information, Rasa can distinguish between New York and Chicago via the departure and destination roles. The role information can also be used in slot mapping in forms.

In the model training phase, the powerful and deep neural network algorithms of Rasa are able to learn how to predict entity roles correctly. So, when users input requests, our bot can recognize the departure and destination.

In the next section, we will introduce entity groups that can be used to solve the grouping issues of entities.

Using entity groups to divide entities into groups

Sometimes, there will be multiple groups of entities, where each group belongs to one subtask. Entities need to be grouped into subtasks based on semantics. Let's take a look at an example of ordering drinks. A customer could order two drinks, where one is a large cup of juice with ice and the other one is a medium cup of soda without ice. User expressions can be versatile, and if entities are not grouped, the bot system won't be able to understand the configurations of the two separate drinks.

Rasa offers the use of entity groups to tackle this challenge. With entity groups, an entity not only has entity type, but it also has group information, which indicates the subtask that it belongs to.

To use entity groups, we need to annotate our training data with the group information along with the entity type. Some sample training data appears as follows:

```
Hi, I'd like to order two drinks. One [large cup]{"entity":
"size", "group": "1"} of [juice]{"entity": "drink",
"group":"1"}. Another one is [medium cup]{"entity": "size",
"group": "2"} of [soda]{"entity": "drink", "group":"2"}. The
former one [with ice]{"entity": "ingredient", "group": "1"},
and the latter one [without ice]{"entity": "ingredient",
"group": "2"}.
```

In the preceding sample data, we annotate `large cup`, `juice`, and `with ice` as group 1. And we annotate `medium cup`, `soda`, and `without ice` as group 2.

With the group information, the action is able to read the entity groups and handle the situation correctly when multiple groups of requests are bundled together.

So far, we have introduced entity roles and entity groups, what problems they can solve, and how to create our training data. In the next section, we will discuss how we can use this information in the dialogue system to complete the functions we want.

Configuring Rasa to use entity roles and groups

The use of entity roles and entity groups requires the involvement of the settings in the domain, story, form, and NLU pipeline. First, let's take a look at how to set them up in the domain.

Updating the entities setting for roles and groups

For an entity that uses the entity role and groups feature, you need to list the roles and groups information in the `entities` of the `domain` file. Here is an example:

```
entities:
    - time
    - ticket_type
    - city:
        roles:
            - departure
            - destination
    - size:
        groups:
            - 1
            - 2
```

In this example, the `city` entity has two roles: `departure` and `destination`. Additionally, the `size` entity has two groups: `1` and `2`.

Next, we discuss how to use entity roles in stories and forms.

Updating forms and stories for roles and groups

Like ordinary entities, you can also use entities with entity role information in forms or stories. The advantage of this is that the system can take different actions according to different entity roles.

Let's imagine the following use case: when a user first informs us of the place of arrival, we ask whether they want to depart from the current city. When the user first informs us of the place of departure, we ask them about the place of arrival. One possible implementation is as follows:

```
stories:
- story: given destination, ask if departure from current city
  steps:
    <-- greet intent and utter_greet are omitted here -->
    - intent: book_ticket
      entities:
        - city: Shanghai
          role: destination
    - action: utter_ask_departure_from_current_city
- story: given departure, ask the destination
  steps:
    <-- greet intent and utter_greet are omitted here -->
    - intent: book_ticket
      entities:
        - city: Beijing
          role: departure
    - action: utter_ask_destination
```

Another way to use entity roles and entity groups is to use them in forms. This method is actually more common. In the ticket booking scenario, we need to distinguish whether the city belongs to the departure or the destination. An effective way is to define the departure and destination slots, and then map the city entity to the departure or destination slot according to the entity role information. One possible implementation is shown in the following code snippet:

```
forms:
  ticket_form:
    city_depart:
      - type: from_entity
        entity: city
        role: departure
    city_dest:
      - type: from_entity
```

```
        entity: city
          role: destination
      date:
        - type: from_entity
          entity: date
```

In `ticket_form`, we define a `city_depart` slot, which will map from an entity if the entity type is `city` and the entity role is `departure`. We also define a `city_dest` slot, which can map from an entity if the entity type is `city` and the entity role is `destination`.

Next, let's learn how to properly configure the pipeline to support entity roles and entity groups.

Components supporting entity roles and entity groups

Although the function of entity roles and entity groups is very powerful, this feature is not in the traditional NER. Therefore, not all algorithms support this feature. Currently, in Rasa 2.2.x, only `DIETClassifier` and `CRFEntityExtractor` support this feature. You need to make sure that if you want to use entity roles and entity groups, the components that support this feature are added into the pipeline. You only need to add the corresponding components to the pipeline without any special settings.

In the next section, we will check our understanding of these concepts in a practical exercise.

Learning by doing – building a ticket and drink booking bot

We have designed this section to enhance your practical understanding. We will create a ticket and drink booking bot based on a homemade toy-level dataset. The robot can simulate the process of booking tickets and drinks for travelers (they will not actually book tickets or drinks).

What are the features of our bot?

By using a combination of entity roles and slot mapping in the form, we can map city entities into departure and destination slots. In this way, the user's request can be successfully processed.

By using entity groups, our bot system can easily group entities into subtasks, which will make it possible to process them.

How can we implement it?

Let's follow the official Rasa project structure:

```
.
├── actions
│   └── actions.py
├── config.yml
├── credentials.yml
├── data
│   ├── stories.yml
│   └── nlu.yml
├── domain.yml
├── endpoints.yml
└── models
```

Let's begin with the train data.

Creating the NLU training data

In our project, all of the training NLU data is stored in the `data/nlu.yml` file. In this file, we need some training data for an intent: `book_ticket`. We will use this intent to express that users want to book a ticket.

Part of the training data content (the full content has already been provided to you in the GitHub repository) is as follows:

```
version: "2.0"
nlu:
  - intent: book_ticket
    examples: |
      - Help me book the ticket
      - Help me book a ticket for departure from [San
Francisco]{"entity": "city", "role": "departure"}
      - Help me book a ticket from [New York]{"entity": "city",
"role": "departure"}
      - Help me order one from [Tomorrow](date)[New York]
```

```
{"entity": "city", "role": "departure"} to [Berlin]{"entity":
"city", "role": " destination"}'s ticket
        - Help me order a [Tomorrow](date) [Berlin]{"entity":
"city", "role": "departure"} to [Paris]{"entity": "city",
"role": " destination"}'s ticket
        - Book me a ticket for [tomorrow](date)
        - Help me book a ticket to [Madrid]{"entity": "city",
"role": "destination"}
```

In the preceding NLU training data, we have created some training examples (with annotations for entity roles and entity groups) to represent the questions that users might ask our bot.

In the next step, we will create the story data for this project.

Creating the story data and rules

Stories and rules are stored in the data/stories.yml file. In order to more easily observe the entity role and entity group information, we will use the rule to map the intent of book_ticket and book_drinks to the corresponding inspect actions. That is to say, the book_ticket intent will trigger the action_ticket_response action, and the book_drinks intent will trigger the action_drink_response action. The specific configuration is as follows:

```
version: "2.0"
stories:
  - rule: handle drink query
    steps:
      - intent: book_drinks
      - action: action_drink_response
  - rule: handle ticket query
    steps:
      - intent: book_ticket
      - action: action_ticket_response
```

Next, we will talk about the configuration of the domain.

Configuring the domain

The domain settings are stored in the `domain.yml` file. In this chapter, the settings are essentially the same as those that were introduced in previous chapters. We need to add all the slots and entities that are used by the knowledge base actions. The outline of the domain file is as follows:

```
intents:
  <-- we have omitted all the intents here. -->
entities:
  - city:
      roles:
        - departure
        - destination
  - date
  - ingredient:
      groups:
        - 1
        - 2
  - size:
      groups:
        - 1
        - 2
  - drink:
      groups:
        - 1
        - 2 slots:
  <-- we have omitted all the slots here. -->
responses:
  <-- we have omitted all the responses here. -->
actions:
  - action_drink_response
  - action_ticket_response
  <-- we have omitted other actions here. -->
```

In the next step, we will configure the pipelines and policies for Rasa.

Configuring the pipelines and polices

The configurations of the pipelines and policies are stored in the `config.yml` file. In this project, the pipeline settings and policy configurations are nothing special. The complete content of `config.yml` is as follows:

```
language: en
pipeline:
  - name: WhitespaceTokenizer
  - name: LanguageModelFeaturizer
    model_name: bert
    model_weights: "rasa/LaBSE"
  - name: "DIETClassifier"  # supports entity roles and groups
    epochs: 100
    learning_rate: 0.001
policies:
  - name: MemoizationPolicy
  - name: TEDPolicy
  - name: RulePolicy
```

In the NLU pipeline, you should notice that we use `DIETClassifier` to act as an NER extractor. This setting is on purpose. We need a component that supports entity roles and entity groups.

In the next section, we'll examine how to use entity roles and entity groups in custom actions.

Creating our form action

For this toy project, we will not actually call the API to book tickets. Our action only prints out the booking information for us to inspect the entity roles and entity groups. The specific implementation code for `action_ticket_response` is as follows:

```
class TicketQueryAction(Action):
    def name(self) -> Text:
        return "action_ticket_response"


    def run(self, dispatch, tracker, domain):
        entities = []
        for entity in tracker.latest_message['entities']:
```

```
        entities.append(
            {"entity": entity["entity"], "value":
entity["value"],
                "role": entity.get("role")})
        msg = str(entities) + "\n"


        dispatch.utter_message(msg)
        return []
```

The specific implementation code for `action_drink_response` is as follows:

```
class DrinkQueryAction(Action):
    def name(self) -> Text:
        return "action_drink_response"
    def run(self, dispatch, tracker,domain):
        # print out entities by group
        msg = ""
        entities = []
        for entity in tracker.latest_message['entities']:
            if entity.get("group") == "1":
                entities.append(
                    {"entity": entity["entity"], "value":
entity["value"],
                        "group": entity["group"]})
        msg += "group #1: " + str(entities) + "\n"
        entities = []
        for entity in tracker.latest_message['entities']:
            if entity.get("group") == "2":
                entities.append(
                    {"entity": entity["entity"], "value":
entity["value"],
                        "group": entity["group"]})
        msg += "group #2: " + str(entities)
        dispatch.utter_message(msg)
        return []
```

So far, we have completed all of the configuration and coding work. The next step is to train the model and run the system to start the inference.

Training a model, starting the server, and making inferences

We can use the default command for training. Type this into your Terminal (or Command Prompt for Windows):

```
rasa train
```

When the command is over, our model will be placed inside the models directory.

Next, we will run the system. There are two servers that we need to run, that is, the Rasa action server and the Rasa server:

1. Let's begin by running the Rasa action server. We can use the following command to run the Rasa action server:

    ```
    rasa run actions
    ```

    Note that since it is a server, it will not finish running until we close it on purpose.

2. Next, we will start the Rasa server. In a new Terminal, we run rasa shell, which we mentioned in previous chapters. Here, rasa shell is a convenient tool. It not only runs the Rasa server in the background, but it also provides a Terminal-based interactive UI for the user to make inferences. Running rasa shell is easy. Just type the following command into your Terminal:

    ```
    rasa shell
    ```

    After the model has been loaded by rasa shell, we can interact with the bot in the shell command line.

3. Now we can observe the entity role information by entering the corresponding request, as follows:

    ```
    Your input -> Help me order a ticket from Berlin to Paris
    tomorrow
    ```
    ```
    [{'entity': 'city', 'value': 'Berlin', 'role':
    'departure'}, {'entity': 'city', 'value': 'Paris',
    'role': ' destination'}, {'entity': 'date', 'value':
    'tomorrow', 'role': None}]
    ```

As you can see from the output of the bot, it has successfully identified the type of entity, the role of the entity, and has extracted the value of the entity.

4. To inspect the entity group information, you can use following query:

```
Your input ->  One large cup of juice . Another one is
medium cup of soda. The former one with ice, and the
latter one without ice
group #1: [{'entity': 'size', 'value': 'large cup',
'group': '1'}, {'entity': 'drink', 'value': 'juice',
'group': '1'}, {'entity': 'ingredient', 'value': 'with
ice', 'group': '1'}]
group #2: [{'entity': 'size', 'value': 'medium cup',
'group': '2'}, {'entity': 'drink', 'value': 'soda',
'group': '2'}, {'entity': 'ingredient', 'value': 'without
ice', 'group': '2'}]
```

As you can see from the output of the bot, it has successfully identified the groups of entities and output the information of the entities by group.

Congratulations! Thanks to the step-by-step explanation in this section, you have mastered how to use entity roles and entity groups to handle complex NER.

Summary

In this chapter, we introduced entity roles and entity groups. First, we discussed why we need entity roles and entity groups. Second, we examined how to create NLU training data for entity roles and entity groups. Third, we introduced how to configure NLU and dialogue management systems so that we can use entity roles and entity groups. Finally, we built a ticket and drink booking bot, step by step, to help you understand those concepts better.

In the next chapter, we will discuss how Rasa works and examine how to extend (that is, customize) Rasa's functions.

8

Working Principles and Customization of Rasa

In this chapter, we introduce the working principles behind Rasa. We will discuss exactly what happens after Rasa receives requests from its users. This is essential for you to understand how to debug a Rasa application, which we will discuss in *Chapter 11, Debugging, Optimization, and the Community Ecosystem*.

We will also learn how to extend and customize Rasa. Using detailed examples, you will learn to create and use custom components that allow you to use adapters or advanced features not included in Rasa. This will help you to create highly customized or complex chatbot applications.

In this chapter, we will cover the following topics:

- Understanding Rasa's **Natural Language Understanding** (NLU) module
- Understanding Rasa policies
- Writing Rasa extensions
- Practice: Creating your own custom English tokenizer

Understanding Rasa's NLU module

Let's start by looking at how the components in Rasa's NLU module work. We will introduce them separately in their two working processes, namely the training process and the inference process.

How does the NLU training work?

The main implementation of the training process is in the `rasa.nlu.train.train` function and the `rasa.nlu.model.Trainer` class. In this section, we introduce how Rasa's NLU module works during the training process.

Initializing the trainer object

The instantiation step is implemented in the `rasa.nlu.model.Trainer.__init__ ()` method. During the training process, Rasa reads the pipeline field in the `config. yaml` configuration file, and gets the detailed definition of every component in the pipeline.

Rasa takes the component configuration and pipeline configuration as the parameters to call the `create()` class method of the component. This method returns an instance of this class.

In this way, we can create the component instances one by one according to the defined order in the pipeline and put them into a list. This list is also called the pipeline object.

Starting the training process

The training process is implemented in the `rasa.nlu.model.Trainer.train()` method. `Trainer` first updates the context (the variables passed between components) of the pipeline, and then calls the `train()` method in each component. The training process of each component is completed by its own `train()` method.

The `train()` method of a component takes the training data and model configuration as parameters. Besides this, the `train()` method also receives the context from upstream components through `**kwargs` in the parameter list. This context contains the different variables passed by other components. Each component can read and write the context to obtain information from other components or pass information to other components.

Saving the model to disk

After the training process is done, the output model needs to persist to the filesystem. The persistence process is implemented in the `rasa.nlu.model.Trainer.persist()` method. When `Trainer` completes the training processes of all the components, `Trainer` will call the `persist()` method of each component one by one according to their order in the pipeline.

The `persist()` method of a component takes a filename (the trainer will automatically generate a unique filename for each component based on the component name and sequence in the pipeline) and the model output directory path as parameters. The persisting process of each component is completed by its own `persist()` method.

Besides persisting the component, the `persist()` method of a component also needs to return a dictionary that will be used to update the metadata of the component. The trainer records the metadata of all the components. This metadata will be used when loading Rasa models from the filesystem. After the persistence process is done for all the components, `Trainer` writes the pipeline object and metadata of all the components as the model metadata into the model output directory.

How does NLU inference work?

The inference step is implemented in the `rasa.core.interpreter.RasaNLUInterpreter` class and the `rasa.nlu.model.Interpreter` class. In this section, we introduce how Rasa's NLU module works during the inference step.

Initializing the interpreter object

During the inference step, the model needs to be loaded from the filesystem and instantiated again. As we discussed in the previous section, during the training step the trainer already writes all of the metadata into the model directory, and this metadata contains all of the required information to load a model from the filesystem.

Rasa calls the `load()` static method of `rasa.nlu.model.Interpreter` with the directory of the model as a parameter. The `load()` method completes the loading of the model metadata, and then calls the `create()` static method with the metadata and model directory as parameters. In `create()`, use metadata to load each component class in the pipeline, and call the `load()` class method of each component with the component metadata, model directory, and context as parameters. The `load()` method of each component is responsible for restoring itself from the filesystem. Finally, call the `__init__` method of `rasa.nlu.model.Interpreter` with components, context, and model metadata as parameters, to create an `Interpreter` object.

Doing the inference process

The NLU parsing part of the user's request is completed by the `parse()` method of the interpreter. The `parse()` method creates a `message` object which is used to carry data, then calls the `process()` method of each component with the message object and context as the parameters. The inference process of each component is completed by its own `process()` method, and adds the inference result to the message object. After the last component inference is completed, the message object contains all of our inference results.

Constructing the output result

The final output of the inference is based on the data in the message object.

It is worth noting that when constructing the output result from the message object, it will filter the data according to the configuration. When you implement your own custom component, you need to add data to the message object through the `set()` method of the message object, and make sure to set the `add_to_output` parameter to `True`.

Here is an example of the final NLU inference results:

```json
{
    "text": "What's the weather like tomorrow for New York?",
    "intent": {
        "name": "weather_inquiry",
        "confidence": 0.95
    },
    "entities": [
        {
            "start": 4,
            "end": 5,
            "value": "tomorrow",
            "entity": "date",
        },
        {
            "start": 6,
            "end": 8,
            "value": "New York",
            "entity": "city",
        }
```

```
        ]

    }
```

We introduced the output format of NLU in *Chapter 2, Natural Language Understanding in Rasa*. So, you should be familiar with each field in the preceding example.

As we come to the end of this section, you should now have a deeper understanding of how these results are processed. In the following section, we will discuss how Rasa policies work.

Understanding how Rasa policies work

It is important to understand how Rasa policies work. By being familiar with their working principles, developers can debug the dialogue management function.

Using historical context is very important for a policy to predict the next action. Suppose our bot can book train tickets and plane tickets. There is a conversation that has been going on for multiple turns. In the last turn, when the bot asked the user where the departure point was, the user replied: "New York." If there is no historical information, our bot will not know whether it is currently booking a train ticket or a plane ticket. Therefore, the next action cannot be determined. Policies in Rasa normally use multiple history states (five by default).

It is crucial for Rasa's dialogue management module to turn those history states into some data structures that a policy can use. This conversion is the topic we will discuss in the next section.

Converting trackers to training data

The dialogue history in Rasa is stored in the tracker object. A tracker represents the whole dialogue history between a user and the bot. This is true for both the training and inference processes.

Converting a tracker to training data requires several steps, which we will discuss in the following subsections.

Converting from a tracker to a prior tracker

During training and inference, we need to extract the historical dialogue state from the conversation. The status of a historical dialogue can be represented by a prior tracker. A prior tracker records the history from the beginning of the conversation to a certain turn in history. We can generate a series of prior trackers from a tracker.

The `generate_all_prior_trackers()` method of the `rasa.shared.core.trackers.DialogueStateTracker` class is the key to generate prior trackers from a tracker. The conversation history is stored in the tracker object. History is stored in Rasa using events. Each event represents what happened in the past. Rasa generates the prior tracker from the tracker by replaying these events.

The generation process is shown in the following figure:

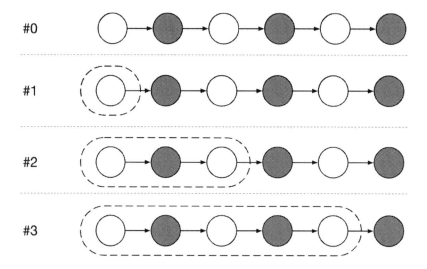

Figure 8.1 – The process of generating prior trackers

In the preceding figure, **#1**, **#2**, and **#3** represent the three prior trackers that are generated by tracker **#0**.

Each dialogue history can be categorized into two types of events: `ActionExecuted` events and `non-ActionExecuted` events. The `ActionExecuted` event is the execution of a Rasa action, represented as a gray circle. The `Non-ActionExecuted` event is for all events except `ActionExecuted` events, which are represented by white circles. Every time an `ActionExecuted` event is encountered, a prior tracker is generated. *Figure 8.1* is just a simplified demonstration, and in a real scenario, Rasa will execute multiple actions consecutively, so there will be multiple `ActionExecuted` events.

Converting from a prior tracker to a tracker state

A prior tracker represents the dialogue state and cannot be used directly by the algorithms to predict the next actions. To do this, we need first to convert a prior tracker to a tracker state. In the context of a policy, a tracker state is a dictionary with the feature name as the dictionary key and the feature value as the dictionary value.

The get_active_state() method of the rasa.shared.core.domain. Domain class is the key to convert prior trackers to tracker states. The key conversation information recorded in the prior tracker (intent and entities status, current slot's status, active loop status, and actions status) will be converted into the tracker state.

Here we give a brief description of the conversion process. When converting the intent and entities to a tracker state, Rasa extracts the intent name and the entity type (with role and group, if any) of the last turn as the state. Rasa extracts the slot name as the key, and the slot feature (by slot.as_feature()) as the value, to create a directory for the slot's status. For active_loop, Rasa extracts the value of the last active loop (the name of a form) as the state. For the actions status, Rasa extracts the last action as the state.

Here is an example of a tracker state:

```
{
    'user': {
        'intent': 'weather',
        'entities': ('date-time',)
    },
    'slots': {'address': (1.0,)},
    'prev_action': {'action_name': 'weather_form'},
    'active_loop': {'name': 'weather_form'}
}
```

In this tracker state, the user key is used to store the status of intent and entity, the slots key is used to store slot states, the prev_action key is used to store previous action states, and the active_loop key is used to store the active loop status.

Tracker states can be directly input into basic policies like memorization. But for advanced policies, the tracker state needs further processing before it can be used. We will discuss this topic in the following subsections.

Padding and truncating of the tracker state

Conversations can have different lengths. This will result in a different number of tracker states being converted from different trackers. Models based on machine learning can usually only process fixed-length inputs. It is essential to pad or truncate the original tracker state to get a fixed-length input.

`TrackerFeaturizer` in Rasa handles this padding and truncation function. According to different ways of handling maximum length, `TrackerFeaturizer` has two subclasses: `FullDialogueTrackerFeaturizer` and `MaxHistoryTrackerFeaturizer`. `FullDialogueTrackerFeaturizer` uses the whole dialogue history as features to predict the next action. In contrast, `MaxHistoryTrackerFeaturizer` only uses the most recent *N* turns of dialogue history to predict the next action.

`MaxHistoryTrackerFeaturizer` is based on the fact that dialogue context has strong locality. Locality means that the information needed for the current context should in most cases be within the most recent several turns of dialogue. In other words, the very old dialogue content should have little or no impact on the current dialogue state.

Here is a demonstration of how `MaxHistoryTrackerFeaturizer` works:

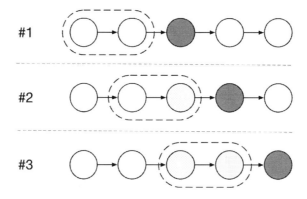

Figure 8.2 – Max history tracker

Figure 8.1 shows the working process of training `MaxHistoryTrackerFeaturizer` with `max_history` set to be 2. The gray node refers to the current turn. The white nodes before the gray node refer to the history turns. We can see that although **#2** and **#3** both have more than two turns of history dialogue (since `max_history` is set to be 2), only the most recent two turns of history dialogue will be used.

More advanced policies (such as `TEDPolicy`) cannot use a tracker state directly. First, it needs to be converted into more detailed numerical values. We will discuss this process in the next section.

Converting a tracker state to a tracker state feature

The `SingleStateFeaturizer` class of the `rasa.core.featurizers.single_state_featurizer` module is the key class used to process the conversion from a tracker state to a tracker state feature. Different types of dialogue information will be converted in different ways. Most types of dialogue information are encoded to one-hot or multi-hot features.

In this example, we provide a simplified demonstration of the tracker state feature:

```
{
    "intent": [0, 0, 0, 1, 0, 0, 0, 0, 0, 0],
    "entities": [1, 0],
    "action_name": [1, 0, 0, 0, 0],
}
```

From this demonstration of the tracker state feature, we know that all dialogue information is converted to a fixed-length numerical vector feature.

How does policy training work?

In Rasa, policy training data will be treated as multiple trackers. Each tracker stores a complete story. In the training process, we extract the tracker state feature from the tracker and predict the next action. This is a typical supervised learning task. The task of the policy becomes the typical time series classification problem. The specific algorithm varies greatly from component to component. You can refer to the documentation of each component to understand how their algorithms work.

How does policy inference work?

When we start a new conversation, the tracker state is not completely empty. If a user starts a new conversation, `action_session_start` will automatically run to add `action_listen` as the executed action into the tracker.

The dialogue management module runs in a similar way to training a model. It constantly tracks the dialogue state and provides features to the relevant policy. The policy predicts and runs actions until the action is to wait for user input (`ActionListen`) or the maximum number of actions is exceeded (to avoid deadlocks).

Writing Rasa extensions

Rasa is very flexible for extensions. Besides using the built-in functions, developers can freely extend it to have third-party functions.

There are two common scenarios for using custom components. The first scenario is to develop a custom adapter. Rasa and many **Instant Messaging systems (IMs)** can communicate with each other through the built-in connector, but if the IM used by the user is not supported (usually a product with fewer users or a private product), you can create an adapter for it yourself. The second scenario is to develop custom NLU or dialogue management components. Technology is developing rapidly in the field of chat robots, and most senior developers use their own models or techniques in their projects.

First of all, let's discuss how to write pipeline and policy extensions.

Writing pipeline and policy extensions

In practical applications, the probability of using custom pipeline components is much greater than using custom strategies. The usage method and implementation steps of a custom strategy are similar to those of a custom pipeline component. In this example, we mainly focus on introducing how to customize the pipeline components.

In the configuration of the Rasa pipeline, developers can directly use the built-in component name to refer to the component. This is shown in the following example:

```
pipeline:
  - name: WhitespaceTokenizer
  - name: LanguageModelFeaturizer
    model_name: "bert"
    model_weights: "rasa/LaBSE"
  - name: DIETClassifier
    epochs: 100
    learning_rate: 0.001
```

In the example, `WhitespaceTokenizer`, `LanguageModelFeaturizer`, and `DIETClassifier` are the names of built-in components.

The method of finding components by name cannot be applied to custom components, because Rasa does not establish a mapping relationship between the name and the custom component code. Thanks to the flexibility of Python, Rasa supports loading custom components dynamically. For example, we have a component called AwesomeLanguageModelFeaturize. It has the same function as LanguageModelFeaturizer. This component (a class) is located in the mod module of the pkg package. We can use this component with its fully qualified name (a dotted name showing the path from the package to a class, function, or method). In our case, the fully qualified name of the component is pkg.mod. AwesomeLanguageModelFeaturizer. The following is an example of the use of this custom component:

```
pipeline:
  - name: WhitespaceTokenizer
  - name: pkg.mod.AwesomeLanguageModelFeaturizer
    model_name: "bert"
    model_weights: "rasa/LaBSE"
  - name: DIETClassifier
    epochs: 100
    learning_rate: 0.001
```

In this example configuration, we used a custom component called pkg. mod.AwesomeLanguageModelFeaturizer to replace the built-in LanguageModelFeaturizer component. The configuration method of custom components is the same as that of built-in components. In this example, we passed two parameters: model_name and model_weights.

The specific implementation of the custom component depends on the function to be implemented. Rasa provides a base class for each type of component. By inheriting the base class, developers can create custom components more efficiently. We will teach you how to create a working tokenizer component in the exercise part at the end of this chapter.

In the next section, we will discuss how to write custom slot types.

Writing custom slot types

The developer can create a custom slot type if the built-in slot type cannot meet the needs of a given situation. Let's take a restaurant reservation system as an example. The reservation system reserves small tables or large tables according to the number of diners. Assume that the reservation rule is: if the number of diners is four or less, a small table is reserved; if the number of diners is more than four and less than eight, a large table is reserved; if there are more than eight diners, the reservation system cannot handle this situation and the reservation will fail. The reservation system needs to perform different operations according to different table reservations. The built-in slot type cannot handle this situation, so we need to create a custom slot type.

The easiest way to create a custom slot is to inherit the slot base class (`rasa.shared.core.slots.Slot`) and override the `_feature_dimensionality()` and `_as_feature()` methods. The `_feature_dimensionality()` method is used to return the dimension (number) of the feature. The `_as_feature()` method converts the value of slot (in most cases from the entity) into a feature in numerical form (the dimension needs to be consistent with the return value of the `_feature_dimensionality()` method). One possible implementation of the slot type is as follows:

```python
from rasa.shared.core.slots import Slot


class TableSlot(Slot):
    type_name = "table"

    def _feature_dimensionality(self):
        return 3

    def _as_feature(self):
        r = [0.0] * self._feature_dimensionality()
        if self.value:
            if self.value <= 4:
                r[0] = 1.0
            elif self.value <= 8:
                r[1] = 1.0
            else:
                r[2] = 1.0
        return r
```

In this implementation, the reservation status of the table converts to a feature in a way similar to one-hot encoding. The detailed conversation is as follows: if the number of diners is not given (this slot is not used), the slot feature is (0, 0, 0). If a small table is reserved (the number of diners is less than or equal to four), the slot feature is (1, 0, 0). If a large table is reserved (the number of diners is greater than four and less than or equal to eight), the slot feature is (0, 1, 0). If the number of diners exceeds eight, the slot feature is (0, 0, 1).

The slot system allows developers to output different feature dimensions according to slot configuration, and this is the reason that `feature_dimentionality()` is a method instead of an attribute. Developers need to make sure that if there is no change in the configuration, the dimension of the model output feature should stay the same, otherwise, the inconsistency of feature dimensions in the training process and inference process will cause system errors.

It is worth noting that the slot can output different feature dimensions according to the configuration, and this is why the slot outputs the feature dimension through a method (`_feature_dimentionality()`) instead of an attribute.

Writing extensions for other functionalities

In addition to using custom NLU components and policies, Rasa also supports custom data loading (via custom data importer), custom tracker stores, custom connectors, and so on. Since those functions are rarely used, we do not discuss them further in this chapter. If you are interested in this functionality, you can read the documentation and code.

Practice – Creating your own custom English tokenizer

As we discussed in the previous section, Rasa has a powerful extension system, and this allows you to create custom components. In this section, we will show you how to create an English tokenizer.

As discussed in *Writing Rasa extensions*, the easiest way to create a custom component is to inherit the base class provided by Rasa. For our tokenizer, it needs to inherit `rasa.nlu.tokenizers.tokenizer.Tokenizer`, and override the `tokenize()` method.

For the sake of simplicity, we will use a simple way to split English text into tokens: splitting the text according to spaces. One possible implementation of our English tokenizer is as follows:

```
from rasa.nlu.tokenizers.tokenizer import Tokenizer


class MyWhitespaceTokenizer(Tokenizer):
    def __init__(self, component_config):
        super().__init__(component_config)

    def tokenize(self, message, attribute):
        text = message.get(attribute)

        words = text.split()

        tokens = self._convert_words_to_tokens(words, text)

        return self._apply_token_pattern(tokens)
```

In this implementation, we do the following:

1. We first get the text from the message.
2. Next, we split the text into token strings based on the spaces, since the expected output of the tokenizer is a list of token objects.
3. Then we call the `_convert_words_to_tokens()` method of the base class to convert the token strings into a list of token objects.
4. We apply the token pattern to `tokens`. The token pattern is a regular expression that splits a token into multiple tokens. This is a common feature of all tokenizers.
5. Finally, we call the `_apply_token_pattern()` function of the base class to achieve this feature.

Now let's use the custom English tokenizer component. We have already introduced how to use custom components in the NLU pipeline in the previous section. To test our custom tokenizer, we reuse the weather forecast bot project that has been introduced in *Chapter 4*, *Handling Business Logic*. Replace the `WhitespaceTokenizer` component with the custom English word segmentation component we just created. The modified NLU pipeline is as follows:

```
pipeline:
  - name: customed.tokenizer.MyWhitespaceTokenizer
  - name: LanguageModelFeaturizer
    model_name: "bert"
    model_weights: "rasa/LaBSE"
  - name: RegexFeaturizer
  - name: DIETClassifier
    epochs: 100
    learning_rate: 0.001
  - name: ResponseSelector
    epochs: 100
    learning_rate: 0.001
  - name: EntitySynonymMapper
  - name: FallbackClassifier
```

In this pipeline configuration, we replaced the `WhitespaceTokenizer` component with the fully qualified name of the custom English tokenizer (`customed.tokenizer.MyWhitespaceTokenizer`). The rest remains unchanged.

At the end of the exercise, we train the model, start the action server, and use the Rasa shell to test whether the custom component is working properly. The following shows a conversation between us and the bot:

```
Your input ->  what's the weather today?
Where?
Your input ->  Tokyo
The weather of Tokyo for today (2021-08-04) is broken clouds,
its temperature range is : 26.84°C-33.51°C.
```

From the preceding dialogue, we know that the custom English tokenizer component is working correctly.

Summary

In this chapter, we discussed how Rasa works. Rasa can be divided into two parts: NLU and policies. The key part of NLU is a pipeline composed of components. The core work of the strategy is to convert the tracker into input data that can be used in the model and then train the model. We also introduced how to write Rasa extensions for various functions. Finally, we showed you how to create and use a custom English tokenizer through a practical project.

In the next chapter, we will discuss testing and production deployment in Rasa.

Section 3: Best Practices

In this section, you will learn how to deploy the Rasa system to the production environment with high performance and high scalability. You will also learn how to use conversation-driven development patterns and tools to develop chatbots. Finally, you will learn about some nice tools/libraries from the Rasa ecosystem that can help you improve your development efficiency.

This section comprises the following chapters:

- *Chapter 9, Testing and Production Deployment*
- *Chapter 10, Conversation-Driven Development and Interactive Learning*
- *Chapter 11, Debugging, Optimization, and the Community Ecosystem*

9

Testing and Production Deployment

In this chapter, we will introduce how to test Rasa projects. We will then discuss how to verify NLU data and stories, as well as how to evaluate the performance of NLU models and Dialogue management models. Through testing, we can find errors in projects as early as possible. We can also comprehensively evaluate the performance of bots.

Moving on, we will discuss how to deploy Rasa applications in production environments. We will discuss the choice of deployment methods, model storage, tracker stores, and locker stores. By properly deploying Rasa applications, we can implement model version management, load balancing, service expansion, and other functions in production environments.

We will cover the following topics:

- Testing Rasa projects
- Deploying your Rasa assistant to production

Let's talk about validation and evaluation first, because they are executed before deployment in the software development process.

Testing Rasa projects

In this section, we will start by discussing how to validate data and stories. This step is used to find obvious bugs. Later, we will discuss how to evaluate NLU performance and how to read the corresponding reports. Finally, we will introduce the test story format and learn how to use test stories to evaluate the performance of Dialogue management.

Validating data and stories

If developers can quickly detect whether there are errors and where these potential errors are in NLU data and stories, this can help developers greatly improve work efficiency. In Rasa, there is a command for this purpose:

```
rasa data validate
```

The preceding command will detect errors in the data and configuration. Common errors include the following:

- Inconsistency of the training data (the same training data appearing in two or more different intents)

- The intents in the training data being inconsistent with the intents in the domain file (fewer or more intents)

In addition, this command can also check for conflicts in the story, such as the same story history appearing (the length of the story history depends on the `--max-history` parameter) with different follow-up actions. As we learned in *Chapter 8, Working Principles and Customization of Rasa*, the prediction of Rasa policy is completely dependent on the history of the story, so this conflict will cause the model to fail to predict an action correctly.

In general, the `rasa data validate` command can help us discover some common errors in advance. However, because `rasa data validate` does not run the model, it is impossible to evaluate the actual performance of the model. So, we need more powerful tools to do this. We will discuss these in the next section.

Evaluating the NLU performance

Generally, when performing machine learning, a dataset is divided into a training set and a test set (sometimes a validation or a development set is also created). We use the training set to train the model and let the model learn how to use features to make predictions. We use the test set (usually composed of samples that the model has never seen before, that is, samples not in the training set) to evaluate whether the model uses features correctly and accurately so that it can correctly process data that it has never seen before. This is to determine whether it has good generalization.

Splitting the dataset

Usually, we divide the dataset into the training set and test set in a random manner to ensure that the two data distributions are, as far as possible, the same. Rasa provides us with a convenient command to split the dataset into a training set and test set:

```
rasa data split nlu
```

The preceding command will read the nlu data (by default, this is located in the data directory and you can specify it by using the --nlu parameter). It uses 80% (this is a default value, but you can specify a custom ratio by using the --training-fraction parameter) of the data as training data, and the rest of the data is used as the test set. The newly generated training set and test set will be saved in the directory specified by the --out parameter (by default, it is the train_test_split directory). By default, your new training data will be located at train_test_split/training_data.yml, and your new test data will be located at train_test_split/test_data.yml.

Now that you have the test data, after you train your model with new training data, you can use the test data to evaluate the NLU performance. This is exactly what we will introduce in the next section.

Evaluating NLU models

To see how your trained NLU model performs on the test data, you can use the following command:

```
rasa test nlu --nlu train_test_split/test_data.yml
```

The train_test_split/test_data.yml file is the test nlu data file that we just generated in the previous section (the *Splitting the dataset* section).

After the test command is executed, you will find all the test result files located in the results directory. Different NLU pipelines can have different result files, but all pipelines will include two files: intent_errors.json and intent_report.json.

The intent_errors.json file will report all the failed NLU samples in the test data. The following is a sample error:

```
[
  {
    "text": "Now [tomorrow] (date-time)",
    "intent": "info_date",
    "intent_prediction": {
      "name": "weather",
```

```
            "confidence": 0.9606658220291138
        }
    },
<-- we have omitted some similar items here. -->
]
```

In this report, the input text is Now [tomorrow] (date-time), and the true intent is info_date, but our model predicted it as the weather intent with a confidence level of 0.9606658220291138.

The intent_report.json file is used to report the evaluation metrics. The following block shows a sample report:

```
{
    "goodbye": {
        "precision": 1.0,
        "recall": 1.0,
        "f1-score": 1.0,
        "support": 1,
        "confused_with": {}
    },
<-- we have omitted some similar items here. -->
    "accuracy": 0.9615384615384616,
    "macro avg": {
        "precision": 0.9894736842105264,
        "recall": 0.9333333333333332,
        "f1-score": 0.9545945945945945,
        "support": 26
    },
    "weighted avg": {
        "precision": 0.9635627530364371,
        "recall": 0.9615384615384616,
        "f1-score": 0.9582120582120582,
        "support": 26
    }
}
```

The preceding report contains many metrics from different aspects. First, we will introduce the metrics for each intent. The report on intent metrics is as follows:

```
"goodbye": {
    "precision": 1.0,
    "recall": 1.0,
    "f1-score": 1.0,
    "support": 1,
    "confused_with": {}
},
<-- we have omitted some similar items here. -->
```

The preceding report contains the classification metrics for the goodbye intent. It reported that the accuracy of the goodbye intent is 1.0, the recall is 1.0, f1-score is 0.8, and support (number of samples) is 1.

In addition to the metrics for each intent, this report also contains metrics that reflect the overall situation. The following is the content of the overall situation report:

```
"accuracy": 0.9615384615384616,
"macro avg": {
    "precision": 0.9894736842105264,
    "recall": 0.9333333333333332,
    "f1-score": 0.9545945945945945,
    "support": 26
},
"weighted avg": {
    "precision": 0.9635627530364371,
    "recall": 0.9615384615384616,
    "f1-score": 0.9582120582120582,
    "support": 26
}
```

The report contains metrics: overall accuracy, the macro average (unweighted average) of each classification metric, and the weighted average of each classification metric.

So far, we have learned that the rasa nlu test command provides a lot of detailed reports. These are very important for improving the performance of an NLU model.

In the next section, we will discuss how to test the Dialogue model.

Evaluating Dialogue management performance

In Rasa, developers can use the `test` command to evaluate how trained Dialogue models perform on the test stories.

In the following subsection, we will talk about test stories.

Writing test stories

As we all know, to test the performance of a model, we need to provide input data and the results that we expect (ground truth). Each session (each conversation) is composed of multiple single-turn Dialogues. When we test performance at the session level, we need to provide the test system with the input text, the expected NLU parsing results, and the correct Dialogue actions for each turn. In Rasa, there is a special format to contain all this test information. It is based on the ordinary story format. We already introduced this in *Chapter 3, Rasa Core*.

The only difference between a test story and a normal story is that test stories contain the input text (this could be a list of input text). Test stories are designed to be an end-to-end test of the NLU and Dialogue model, so they must include input text. The following block shows some test stories:

```
stories:
- story: A basic story test
  steps:
  - user: |
      hello
    intent: greet
  - action: utter_ask_howcanhelp
  - user: |
      show me [chinese]{"entity": "cuisine"} restaurants
    intent: inform
  - action: utter_ask_location
  - user: |
      in [Paris]{"entity": "location"}
    intent: inform
  - action: utter_ask_price
```

In order to show you the difference in format between the test story and the ordinary story more intuitively, we will list some ordinary stories:

```
stories:
  - story: This is the description of one story
    steps:
      - intent: greet
      - action: action_ask_howcanhelp
      - slot_was_set:
          - asked_for_help: true
      - intent: inform
        entities:
          - location: "New York"
          - price: "cheap"
      - action: action_on_it
      - action: action_ask_cuisine
      - intent: inform
        entityies:
          - cuisine: "Italian"
      - action: restaurant_form
      - active_loop: restaurant_form
```

The different parts of the test story and the normal story have been marked in bold. In general, there are two differences. The first is the different entity list representation formats. The second is the input text, which only exists in the test stories. The entity list and the input text of the test story are integrated (for example, show me [chinese] {"entity": "cuisine"} restaurants), so that the entity can be both accurately represented and used for the evaluation of the NLU model.

Evaluating Dialogue management models

It is easy to evaluate the performance of Dialogue management in Rasa. As you may have guessed, you can use the command-line tool, as follows:

```
rasa test core --stories test_stories.yml --out results
```

In this command, the test_stories.yml file contains the test stories. The reports will output to the results directory. All the failed stories will output to the results/failed_test_stories.yml file.

Deploying your Rasa assistant to production

Here we introduce how to deploy your Rasa assistant to production.

When to deploy

It is common to use the **minimum viable product** or **MVP** strategy during the product development process. MVP is all about building a usable product prototype that fulfills the key requirements in the most efficient and simple way and then iterating to fine-tune the product details.

In Rasa, the official recommendation is that a product can be put into production as an MVP as soon as it can handle the most important (but not *every*) "happy path" of Dialogue. It's recommended to use Rasa X to have early users test the product prototype. This is in order to continuously improve the model until the product prototype reaches the MVP standard and you are ready to deploy it to a production environment.

Deployment options

When we want to deploy a Rasa assistant on a large scale, we normally use solutions based on Kubernetes or OpenShift. Rasa offers some official simple examples to demonstrate deployment in Kubernetes or OpenShift. As this is not a book about DevOps, we will not cover this in detail, and we recommend interested readers check out the official Rasa website. We also recommend reading additional materials on Kubernetes and OpenShift.

For small-scale deployment or single-server deployment, we can use Docker Compose to deploy our Rasa assistant. Interested readers should read more on Docker.

Developers can also start Rasa by directly running the `rasa` command in the command line, the same as what we do in the development phase. However, this is not recommended for the production environment.

Model storage

For single-server cases, we normally choose to store models in local disk drives.

In large-scale deployments, normally, the training process is separate from the production service. Trained models should be stored in a centralized storage system. When needed, the service program can pull the corresponding model to its local environment and automatically deploy it. This is when we need Rasa's functionality of model storage. Rasa supports multiple solutions for dynamic model storage.

HTTP-based model storage

The Rasa server periodically checks for a new model from a specific HTTP server. If there is a new model, the Rasa server will download and deploy it automatically. We only need to configure this in `endpoint.yml`:

```
models:
    url: http://my-server.com/models/default@latest
    wait_time_between_pulls: 10    # by default 100 with unit second
```

By default, the Rasa server tries to check for a new model file (in zipped format) on the HTTP server every 100 seconds. Developers can customize the time interval or set it to be `None`, so the model only gets fetched once. Rasa uses the ETag information from the HTTP server to judge whether the model is updated without downloading the model itself. An HTTP server such as an Apache or NGINX one can provide an ETag header after proper configuration.

Cloud-based model storage

Rasa supports pulling models from **Amazon Simple Storage Service (S3)**, **Google Cloud Storage (GCS)**, and **Microsoft Azure Storage**. We only cover the configuration of S3 here since the S3 protocol is supported by many distributed storage systems and online service providers and has a large application ecosystem and user community. Rasa NLU handles cloud storage in a very similar way in GCS and Azure, so an introduction to S3 can act as a good reference for GCS and Azure as well.

Dependencies installation

We install the S3 client first:

```
pip install boto3
```

Configuration

We will configure how Rasa connects to the S3 server through the following environment variables:

- AWS_SECRET_ACCESS_KEY
- AWS_ACCESS_KEY_ID
- AWS_DEFAULT_REGION

- BUCKET_NAME (if the bucket named BUCKET_NAME does not exist, Rasa will create one for you)

- AWS_ENDPOINT_URL

A common way to set environment variables is to write the name and value of the environment variable directly before the command to be executed in the command line. The following is an example:

```
ENV_VAR_A=value_a ENV_VAR_B=value_b cmd
```

In this example, the command to be executed is cmd. We set two environment variables for this command: ENV_VAR_A and ENV_VAR_B. The values of these two environment variables are value_a and value_b, respectively.

Usage

After configuring the preceding environment variables, when using commands such as rasa shell, rasa run, and rasa x, developers can add --remote-storage aws to configure pulling models from S3. Rasa will download the zipped model file from cloud storage, unzip it to a temporary file path, and start the service in that path. Here we give an example command:

```
rasa run --model 20210804-024016.tar.gz --remote-storage aws
```

In this example, we set the model storage to be S3-based cloud storage. Rasa will download and run the specified model from cloud storage.

Tracker stores

All of the Dialogue processes within Rasa are stored by tracker objects. In large-scale industry production systems, load balancing and auto-scaling are normally used. User messages are likely to be sent to different servers for handling.

We should store user Dialogue history in an independent place. When a user request reaches the server, the storage service will download the target user's Dialogue history. When the user request ends, the user's Dialogue history should be automatically stored in the storage service. The next time that the user's request reaches the server (it may be a different server instance next time), the storage service will again restore the user's Dialogue history into the system.

This component is called a **tracker store** in Rasa. Rasa offers many out-of-the-box tracker stores:

- `InMemoryTrackerStore` is the default tracker store for Rasa. It uses computer memory as storage. Data will be lost if the server is restarted. This component cannot be shared among different servers and only acts as the default tracker storage solution for a single server.

- `SQLTrackerStore` stores trackers in a **Structured Query Language** (**SQL**) database. PostgreSQL, Oracle (version > 11.0), and SQLite are databases compatible with `SQLTrackerStore`.

- `RedisTrackerStore` uses Redis (`https://redis.io/`) to store trackers. Redis is an open source, in-memory data structure store. It is often used for the production deployment of Rasa applications.

- `MongoTrackerStore` uses MongoDB to store trackers. MongoDB is a document-oriented NoSQL database.

- `DynamoTrackerStore` uses DynamoDB to store trackers. DynamoDB is a NoSQL database running on **Amazon Web Services** (**AWS**).

If the required tracker store is not provided, Rasa allows developers to implement custom tracker stores. The developer can inherit the `TrackerStore` class and implement the solution for the new tracker store. Detailed definitions can be found in the Rasa official documentation (`https://rasa.com/docs/rasa/tracker-stores#custom-tracker-store`).

Lock stores

As we mentioned before, in large-scale industrial production systems, load balancing and auto-scaling are usually used. User messages are likely to be sent to different servers for processing. This may cause an error in the sequence of processing messages. In order to solve this problem, Rasa introduced lock stores, which are distributed locks used to handle the order of message processing, so that messages are always processed in the correct order.

Rasa provides the following built-in lock stores:

- `InMemoryLockStore` is the default lock store. It only works for single processes and doesn't work for multiple Rasa servers, no matter whether they are deployed in single or multiple servers.

- `RedisLockStore` uses Redis as the storage backend. In production environments, Rasa applications are usually distributed on multiple servers and run in a multi-process manner on each server. `RedisLockStore` implements cross-process and cross-server distributed locks, so this lock store must be used in production deployments.

High-performance settings for Rasa servers and action servers

By default, Rasa servers and action servers only use one worker to process requests. In this way, the advantages of modern CPUs with multiple cores are lost. We can make the Rasa server and action server use multiple workers by changing the settings.

In order to use multiple workers in the action server, we need to set the `ACTION_SERVER_SANIC_WORKERS` environment variable to the desired number of workers.

In order to use multiple workers in the Rasa server, we not only need to set the `SANIC_WORKERS` environment variable to the number of workers we want but also set the tracker store and lock store, which we introduced in the previous section.

Summary

In this chapter, we discussed two very important stages in the development of a Dialogue system: testing and deployment. Testing is very important for us to ensure the intelligence of a Dialogue system. We must find the current problems of the Dialogue system through testing and correct these problems. We also discussed how to deploy Rasa projects to production environments. A real large-scale Dialogue system needs to be accessed by tens of thousands or even millions of users at the same time. Such a Dialogue system must have very good horizontal scalability. Fortunately, Rasa considered these issues at the beginning of the design and provided corresponding solutions. By using a central storage system, tracker store, and lock store, we are able to extend our service smoothly.

In the next chapter, we will discuss a user-centered methodology and the tools required for developing Dialogue systems.

10
Conversation-Driven Development and Interactive Learning

Compared with traditional software development, the challenge of developing a chatbot is far greater. This is largely due to the fact that the user could say anything to the dialogue bot. Of course, as a developer, you cannot cope with all possible situations for your robot. Therefore, it is extremely important to understand your user's queries.

In this chapter, we will introduce a methodology in which to develop a dialogue system called **Conversation-Driven Development** (**CDD**). This methodology improves dialogue robots by observing, summarizing, and modifying the dialogue process. Additionally, we will introduce a tool for CDD: **Rasa X**. In a step-by-step manner, we will learn how to use Rasa X to complete all stages of CDD. Finally, we will also introduce you to **Interactive Learning**, which is a technical solution that allows developers to interact with the dialogue system to test system capabilities and quickly build training data.

Moving ahead, you will learn what CDD is and how it can be used to quickly develop conversational robots. Additionally, you will learn how to quickly improve your dialogue system by using Rasa X. Finally, you will learn how to use interactive learning to test the capabilities of the system and how to use it to fix problems quickly.

In this chapter, in particular, we will cover the following topics:

- Introduction to CDD
- Introduction to Rasa X
- Interactive learning in Rasa

Let's begin by introducing you to CDD.

Introduction to CDD

CDD is a methodology that enables you to develop a dialogue system; it was introduced by the Rasa team. It is an iterative and interactive process: developers observe the behavior of users and improve chatbot performance based on those observations.

CDD involves the following steps:

1. *Sharing your bot*: We should distribute our product prototype for user testing as soon as possible. No matter how hard developers try, users will always have something new to input into the chatbot. Many teams spend months developing chatbots and focusing on conversations that, in reality, users never have.

2. *Reviewing conversations*: We should spend time studying the conversation between users and our chatbot. It is very helpful to study real user conversations at each stage of development (from the prototype to the real product). Far too many teams only focus on simple attributes, such as how many users express certain intentions and so on. Instead, they should spend more time studying application scenarios and user experiences from the collected conversations.

3. *Annotating NLU examples*: Data from real users can improve the performance of the model in the production environment. Therefore, annotating incoming messages is important.

4. *Testing your bot*: Use the whole conversation process as an end-to-end testing case. Professional teams should not publish products without proper testing. When a product is launched, there should be dozens of key end-to-end testing cases to cover the key dialogue paths. **Continuous integration** (**CI**) and **continuous deployment** (**CD**) can help you to make the process easy and reliable.

5. *Tracking progress*: We need to define some methods from the business context to determine whether the chatbot dialogue has completed the work. For example, this can be judged by whether the user performed some specific operations (such as a purchase operation during shopping) or did not perform some specific operations (such as no customer service request after 24 hours).

6. *Fixing problems*: We should study the successful conversations along with the failed conversations. Successful conversations can immediately be used as testing cases. In comparison, failed conversations could reveal that we might need more training data or that there are bugs in the code. By tracking how a chatbot fails, we should be able to gradually understand the root cause and fix the bugs.

CDD is not a linear process like the waterfall model. Developers jump between each of these steps. Over time, CDD can discover the real user's needs and make bots more and more adaptable to them.

In the next section, we will introduce Rasa X, which is a tool that implements CDD.

Introduction to Rasa X

Rasa X is a toolset for CDD and was developed by the Rasa team.

> **The license terms of Rasa X**
>
> Rasa X, as mentioned in this book, refers to **Rasa X Community Edition**. Rasa X is a free, closed source tool that is available to all developers. The use of Rasa X requires you to accept its license terms: `https://storage.googleapis.com/rasa-x-releases/rasa_x_ce_license_agreement.pdf`. Rasa X Community Edition is free for non-commercial use. It is also free for commercial use, as long as you don't provide it as a service (Software as a Service) to others. For more details please refer to the official license.

Installing Rasa X

Rasa X is a tool for production environments, so the official documentation (`https://rasa.com/docs/rasa-x/installation-and-setup/installation-guide`) offers many installation methods (such as local installation, Helm Chart installation, and Docker Compose installation). In this chapter, we will only introduce one of the installation modes that developers often use, that is, local installation.

You can install Rasa X in local mode by using the following command (in Command Prompt or Terminal):

```
pip install rasa-x --extra-index-url https://pypi.rasa.com/simple
```

Once the preceding command has successfully installed Rasa X, it will print a message on the screen to convey that Rasa X was installed successfully.

If you choose to install a Rasa X version, you should be careful to choose a version that is compatible with your current Rasa and Rasa SDK. A compatibility matrix (`https://rasa.com/docs/rasa-x/changelog/compatibility-matrix`) can help you with this.

In the next section, we will discuss how to use it.

Using Rasa X

We will introduce the functionalities of Rasa X with the six steps of CDD (as discussed in the *Introduction to Rasa* section).

Sharing your bot

There are two ways for Rasa X to distribute bots: web-link sharing and external channels.

Web-link sharing is implemented by Rasa X to generate a web link for testing users. Users can open the link with the help of a browser and get a simple chat UI in order to interact with the chatbot:

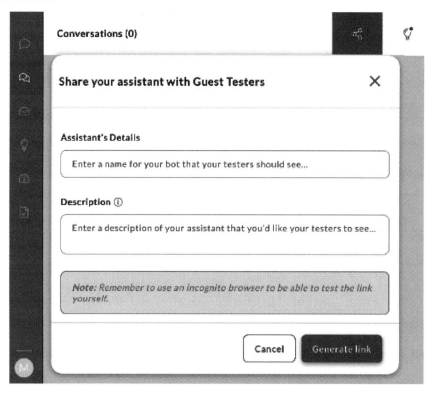

Figure 10.1 – Distributing a chatbot to guest testers

Additionally, Rasa can connect to external clients through channels, which we introduced in *Chapter 3*, *Rasa Core*. Developers can link Rasa to an external client through a channel, and users can directly use the third-party client to interact with the chatbot.

No matter which distribution method we use, Rasa X will be able to record and store a complete dialogue history.

Reviewing conversations

The collected conversation history is stored on the **Conversations** page within Rasa X. Developers can filter, review, and tag conversations on the **Conversations** page. These operations are done on the user interface via the mouse and keyboard, which is very intuitive. You can view an example of the **Conversations** page as follows:

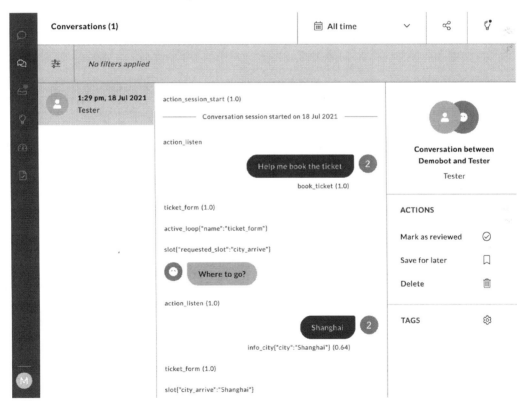

Figure 10.2 – Reviewing conversations

Annotating NLU examples

All of the NLU information during a conversation is recorded on the **NLU Inbox** page within Rasa X. Developers can mark the sentence as correct if the NLU results are right, and if not, developers can correct the records and save them for the purposes of further training. These operations can be carried out through the user interface, as follows:

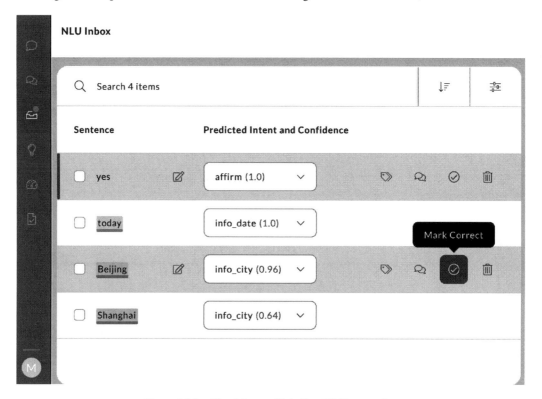

Figure 10.3 – Checking and labeling NLU examples

Testing your bot

All of the conversations are recorded to corresponding end-to-end stories. Developers can choose to save them as end-to-end testing cases. Rasa X will save the story to the directory of tests. Then, developers can run the `rasa test` command to use this end-to-end case to test trained models. These operations can be done through the user interface, as shown in *Figure 10.3*.

Notice that in Rasa X, saving a conversation to a story requires your Rasa X to be connected to a remote Git repository. However, local mode does not support integrated version control. Instead, you can simply copy the test story content (as shown on the right-hand side of *Figure 10.3*) and paste it into your test story file:

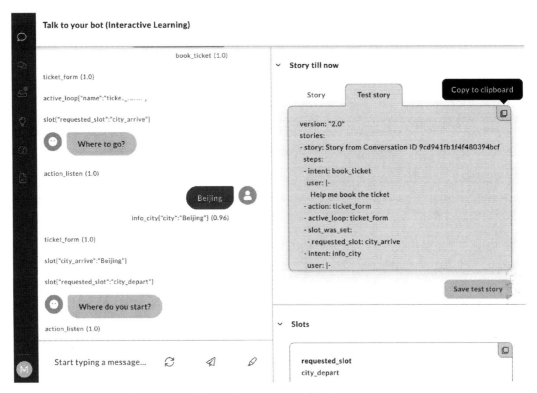

Figure 10.4 – Generating a test story file for a conversation

Tracking progress

Developers need to think about a solution that tracks whether the bot conversations actually address the user's questions. Let's take the example of sales. If the user clicks on the link provided by the chatbot to buy something, the given link should contain the dialogue ID. When the shopping action is done online, a callback link should let the chatbot know that this conversation is successful from both a technical sense and a business sense.

Rasa offers a web-based API to support this. E-commerce systems can use this API to label specific dialogues and use this label to track whether the dialogue is a success or not. For example, you can use the `curl` command to label the conversation (that is, replace {RASA_X_HOST} and {CONVERSATION_ID} with your own values):

```
curl --data '[{"value":" added_to_cart","color":" 228B22"}]'
http://{RASA_X_HOST}/api/conversations/{CONVERSATION_ID}/tags
```

In the preceding command, we will label the conversion (as identified by the conversation ID) to tag `added_to_cart`.

Rasa X also supports labeling dialogues in the backend by hand, so developers can label the dialogue by tracking its content and process.

Fixing problems

The best way to find problems in a conversation is to review and mark them regularly, and then use tag filtering to deal with all kinds of problems one by one. By filtering labels, developers can find conversations that have potential issues. If the issues are caused by NLU extraction, we can add in more training data or fine-tune the component configuration to mitigate them. If the issues are from stories, we can use interactive learning to generate new stories or fine-tune the policies. It is also possible that the issues are from the action server, in which case, we need to debug them according to the situation.

So far, we have discussed the six steps of CDD in Rasa X. In the next section, we will discuss interactive learning.

Interactive learning in Rasa

In interactive learning mode, users can directly interact with the bot and give feedback, and then immediately correct any errors during the process. With interactive learning, we can test our bot prototype on a large scale and easily debug it intuitively.

In Rasa, interactive learning can be done in the Rasa CLI and Rasa X. The Rasa shell is based on the command line, while Rasa X is based on the web user interface. Although the two manifestations are different, under the hood, they are the same interactive learning mechanism. Since Rasa installation comes with the Rasa CLI, we will introduce interactive learning based on the Rasa CLI.

Starting interactive learning

In order to run interactive learning, first, we need to start the Rasa action server:

1. As we have done in the previous chapters, let's start the action server using the following command:

    ```
    rasa run actions
    ```

2. The next step is to begin interactive learning. We briefly introduced several important commands in the *Rasa commandline* section of *Chapter 1, Introduction to Chatbots and Rasa the Framework*. Among them is `rasa interactive`. The `rasa interactive` command is used for interactive learning. The `rasa interactive` command works similarly to `rasa shell`. Both start the Rasa server in the background and then start a command line-based interactive interface on the frontend at the same time.

3. Execute the following command in Command Prompt or Terminal to start interactive learning:

```
rasa interactive
```

This command will load the model. When the loading is complete, it is time to implement interactive learning, which we will discuss in the next section.

Performing interactive learning

Once the `rasa interactive` command has finished the model loading job, we will enter the interactive learning mode. In this mode, Rasa will ask us to confirm the NLU and Core prediction results after each input.

In the following subsections, we will discuss how to confirm the NLU results and the action prediction results.

Confirming the NLU parsing result

After each input, Rasa will ask us to confirm whether the NLU parsing result is correct, as detailed in the following steps:

1. If there is an error in the NLU parsing, whether it is an intent classification error or an entity extraction error, it will enter the error correction step. This requires the user to provide the correct intent classification and entity extraction results in turn.

2. After the user gives the input, Rasa will give the current prediction result (note that this result includes intent classification and entity extraction) and ask whether it is correct. We can choose `Yes` or `No`, as shown in the following code block:

```
? Your input -> What's the weather like tomorrow?
```

```
? Is the intent 'weather' correct for 'What's the weather like
[tomorrow](date-time)?' and are all entities labeled correctly?
(Y/n)
```

If we choose Yes, the confirmation of the intention classification is over. However, if we choose No, then we need to provide Rasa with the correct NLU parsing result. There are two parts to this: providing the correct intent classification result and providing the correct entity extraction result.

3. You can provide the correct intent classification result by selecting from the intent list or creating a new one, as shown in the following code block:

```
? Your input -> What's the weather like tomorrow?

? Is the intent 'weather' correct for 'What's the weather like
[tomorrow](date-time)?' and are all entities labeled correctly?
No
? What intent is it?   (Use arrow keys)

  » <create_new_intent>
    1.00 weather
    0.00 info_date
    0.00 greet
    0.00 goodbye
    0.00 info_address
```

After providing the correct intent classification result, Rasa will ask you to provide the entity extraction result. You can provide the correct entity extraction results using the format we discussed in *Chapter 2, Natural Language Understanding in Rasa*, as shown in the following block:

```
? Your input -> What's the weather like tomorrow?

? Is the intent 'weather' correct for 'What's the weather like
[tomorrow](date-time)?' and are all entities labeled correctly?
No
? What intent is it?   1.00 weather

? Please mark the entities using [value](type) notation What's
the weather like [tomorrow](date-time)?
```

You should note that Rasa has already given the result of automatically parsed entity extraction. You can edit it, as needed, by using the left and right keys to move the cursor.

In the next section, we will discuss how to confirm the action prediction result.

Confirming the action prediction result

After the NLU parsing, the next step is to predict the next action based on the NLU parsing results and other states, such as historical actions and slot conditions (we discussed these in *Chapter 8, Working Principles and Customization of Rasa*).

In interactive learning mode, Rasa will print out the current conversation state for the user to observe before predicting the next action. Then, Rasa will provide the current predicted next action and ask the user to confirm whether it is correct. We can choose Y or n, as shown in *Figure 10.5*:

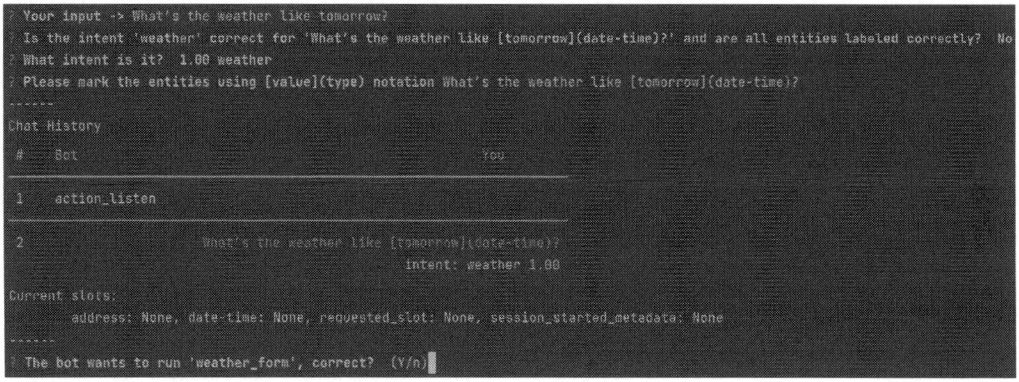

Figure 10.5 – Rasa printing out the current conversation state and waiting for confirmation

If we choose Y, the confirmation of the next action of this timestep is over. However, if we choose n, then we choose the correct next action to execute by selecting it from the action list or creating a new one, as shown in *Figure 10.6*:

```
------
? The bot wants to run 'weather_form', correct?  No
------
Chat History

 #    Bot                                                    You


 1    action_listen


 2                       What's the weather like [tomorrow](date-time)?
                                              intent: weather 1.00

Current slots:
        address: None, date-time: None, requested_slot: None, session_started_metadata: None

------
? What is the next action of the bot?  (Use arrow keys)
» <create new action>
   1.00 weather_form
   0.30 action_default_fallback
   0.00 ...
   0.00 action_back
   0.00 action_deactivate_loop
   0.00 action_default_ask_affirmation
   0.00 action_default_ask_rephrase
   0.00 action_listen
   0.00 action_restart
   0.00 action_revert_fallback_events
   0.00 action_session_start
   0.00 action_two_stage_fallback
   0.00 action_weather_form_submit
   0.00 utter_ask_address
   0.00 utter_ask_date-time
   0.00 utter_default
   0.00 utter_goodbye
   0.00 utter_greet
```

Figure 10.6 – Selecting the next action at the timestep

In each round of interactive learning, confirmation of the NLU analysis results and confirmation of the multiple action prediction results are required. If you are confused about why there are multiple actions, please visit the *How does the policy inference work?* section of *Chapter 8, Working Principles and Customization of Rasa.*

In the next section, we will discuss how to save the data you fed back to the robot during interactive learning into NLU training samples and stories.

Saving the interactive learning data and exiting

The feedback given to the chatbot in interactive learning is not automatically saved as a training sample. The user is required to explicitly export these training samples. This is very easy to do in interactive training mode. Users simply need to press *Ctrl + C* and select whichever options they want. The list of options is as follows:

```
? Do you want to stop?   (Use arrow keys)

 » Continue
   Undo Last
   Fork
   Start Fresh
   Export & Quit
```

After we have selected the `Export & Quit` option, Rasa will ask several questions about where to save the data. After Rasa saves the data to the relevant files, the interactive learning command will end. The whole process is as follows:

```
? Do you want to stop?   Export & Quit

? Export stories to (if file exists, this will append the
stories) data/stories.yml
? Export NLU data to (if file exists, this will merge learned
data with previous training examples) data/nlu.yml
? Export domain file to (if file exists, this will be
overwritten) domain.yml
```

Congratulations, you have made your way through this entire chapter. At this point, you should have a deep understanding of CDD and interactive learning.

Summary

In this chapter, we discussed CDD, which is a methodology that is used to construct dialogue systems efficiently. We introduced a tool for CDD: Rasa X. We explained, in detail, how to use Rasa X to complete the six steps of CDD, that is, sharing, reviewing, annotating, testing, tracking, and fixing. Additionally, we discussed interactive learning and demonstrated, in detail, how to use the Rasa CLI to complete interactive learning. After studying these two topics, you should now have more confidence regarding how to build a successful dialogue system in theory and in practice.

In the next chapter, we will discuss how to debug and optimize the dialogue system and introduce Rasa's open source community ecosystem.

11
Debugging, Optimization, and Community Ecosystem

In this chapter, we will learn how to debug a Rasa application, and how to optimize the Rasa system for our application. We will also cover some tools within the Rasa community ecosystem that can help developers to build chatbots.

You will learn the skills needed to efficiently debug Rasa applications, and by the end of the chapter, you will understand the best practices that can help your Rasa system to achieve better performance. You will also discover some excellent tools that can help to build your chatbots.

In this chapter, we will cover the following topics:

- Debugging Rasa systems
- Optimizing Rasa systems
- Understanding the community ecosystem of Rasa

Debugging Rasa systems

A chatbot is a complex software system. Therefore, we need to design and configure Rasa projects carefully. It is pretty common for developers to get different kinds of bugs when building Rasa-based chatbots. In general, those bugs can be of two types: one is that the prediction results are not as expected; another is that there is a code error in the Rasa system, and the bot cannot run normally. We will cover both types of bugs in the following subsections.

Wrong prediction of results

Two problems may cause the wrong prediction of results. It can be that the **Natural Language Understanding** (**NLU**) module makes the wrong prediction on user intent and entities, or it can be that a policy makes the wrong prediction on the next action. It is crucial to first make sure which of these problems is causing the wrong predictions.

Fortunately, most of the commands in Rasa have the debug function. Developers can turn on the debugging option to obtain critical internal information from Rasa in real time to help debug the system. When we get wrong prediction results, it is recommended to use the built-in `rasa shell` command with the `-vv` flag added to it (that is, `rasa shell -vv`) to turn on debug mode. In the following subsections, we will discuss how to spot NLU parsing errors and action prediction errors.

Finding NLU parsing errors

After a user types an input, the Rasa shell in debug mode will give a detailed NLU parsing result in a log, as shown in the following example:

```
Your input ->  weather in Shanghai
DEBUG    rasa.core.processor  - Received user message 'weather
in Shanghai' with intent '{'id': -8721386961924253444, 'name':
'weather', 'confidence': 0.9982607960700989}' and entities
'[{'entity': 'address', 'start': 11, 'end': 19, 'confidence_
entity': 0.9993818998336792, 'value': 'Shanghai', 'extractor':
'DIETClassifier'}]'
```

In this example, the key pieces of information are intent `'{'id':` `-8721386961924253444, 'name': 'weather', 'confidence':` `0.9982607960700989}'` and entities `'[{'entity':` `'address', 'start': 11, 'end': 19, 'confidence_entity':` `0.9993818998336792, 'value': 'Shanghai', 'extractor':` `'DIETClassifier'}]'`. The former gives intent information, and the latter gives entity information. With this information, you can determine whether there is an error in the NLU parsing.

Finding action prediction errors

After NLU parsing, it is time for Rasa to make action predictions. As we have already discussed in *Chapter 8, Working Principles and Customization of Rasa*, there are many variables (such as NLU analysis results, slot status, dialogue history, and so on) that affect the results of action prediction. Therefore, this information will be printed out by the Rasa shell in debug mode (below the log about the NLU parsing result). This can be seen in the following example:

```
DEBUG    rasa.core.processor  - Current slot values:
          address: None
          date-time: None
          requested_slot: None
          session_started_metadata: None
DEBUG    rasa.core.policies.memoization  - Current tracker
state:
[state 1] user intent: weather | user entities: ('address',) |
previous action name: action_listen
DEBUG    rasa.core.policies.memoization  - There is no
memorized next action
DEBUG    rasa.core.policies.ted_policy  - TED predicted 'utter_
greet' based on user intent.
```

The critical information in the example log is the Current slot values value and the Current tracker state value. It also prints out the policy status. There is no memorized next action, and the TED policy gives the action prediction result utter_greet.

With this information, you can determine whether there is an error in the action prediction.

Code errors

There can be cases where there is an error in the code, and the system throws an exception and stops running. We will then need to debug the Python source code to track the bugs.

In general, there are two options for debugging Python code. One way is to use the built-in Python pdb module, the official solution for Python programs. Although it has a steep learning curve, this method does not require the installation of third-party libraries, and it has a wide range of applications and powerful functions. Therefore, it is very suitable for senior Python developers and online production environments. Another way to debug a Python program is to use a **Graphical User Interface (GUI)**-based **Integrated Development Environment (IDE)**. This method is intuitive and straightforward to use. Compared with pdb, a GUI-based IDE is more friendly to ordinary developers. Therefore, it is suitable for use in the development phase.

In this section, we will introduce these two debugging methods in more detail.

Using the pdb module to debug

The best way to use the pdb module for debugging is to automatically enter the post-mortem debugging mode when an error occurs. Post-mortem debugging is the debugging of the program after it has already crashed. It allows you to quickly find the most direct cause of the error and view the entire call stack at the time of the crash. Let's have a look at this in the following steps:

1. The following is an example of post-mortem debugging using the pdb command (executed in the Command Prompt or terminal):

```
python -m pdb -c continue -m rasa train
```

    The rasa train part of this command is the Rasa command you want to debug.

    Unfortunately, the preceding command is only available in Python 3.7 and later versions (the -m option is newly introduced to the pdb module in Python 3.7). For users of Python before 3.7, you can use the following method instead. The alternative is to directly find the location of the program entry module and enable the pdb debugging function by calling the source code. The entry module for all the Rasa commands is the rasa.__main__ module.

2. You can find the file location of the rasa.__main__ module by executing the following Python code in the Python interpreter:

```
>>> from rasa import __main__ ; print(__main__.__file__)
<XXX>/rasa/__main__.py
```

The preceding command successfully outputs the file location of the Rasa entry module, which is `<XXX>/rasa/__main__.py` (where the `<XXX>` part represents the omitted path prefix).

3. Once you have the file path of the entry module, you can use the following command (executed in the command prompt or terminal) to implement post-mortem debugging:

```
python -m pdb -c continue <XXX>/rasa/__main__.py train
```

In the preceding command, `<XXX>/rasa/__main__.py` is the file path of the Rasa command-line entry module, and the `train` part is the Rasa subcommand we want to execute. In terms of effect, this command is entirely equivalent to the debugging command we have introduced before. The disadvantage of this command is obvious in that it is relatively cumbersome, and the advantage is that it can be used in any Python version.

4. No matter which method you use to start `pdb` debugging, you will enter the `pdb` debugger after an error occurs in the operation of the Rasa command, as shown in the following:

```
Uncaught exception. Entering post mortem debugging
Running 'cont' or 'step' will restart the program
> /<XXX>/Chapter11/customed/tokenizer.py(12)tokenize()
-> raise ValueError("This is an on purpose exception")
(Pdb) <!-- Cursor is blinking here -->
```

In the preceding interface, the `pdb` debugger is waiting for your input.

In the `pdb` debugger, you need to operate the debugger through commands to observe the current program status, control program execution, switch context, or perform another action. Here, we give an example of operating the `pdb` debugger:

```
> /<XXX>/Chapter11/customed/tokenizer.py(12)tokenize()
-> raise ValueError("This is an on purpose exception")
(Pdb) longlist <!-- type your pdb command here -->
  8          def tokenize(self, message, attribute):
  9              text = message.get(attribute)
 10
 11              # raise exception on purpose
 12 ->          raise ValueError("This is an on purpose
exception")
```

```
 13
 14                    words = text.split()
 15
 16                    tokens = self._convert_words_to_tokens(words,
text)
 17
 18                    return self._apply_token_pattern(tokens)
(Pdb) <!-- Cursor is blinking here -->
```

In the preceding example, we used the `longlist` command to print the code of the currently executing function. The line of code currently being executed has been marked in the output with `->` on its left side. In order to highlight this in the code block, the text of this line has been underlined (in the real output, the text is not underlined).

5. We list the commonly used `pdb` debugging commands for you here:

Command	Description
`longlist`	List the source code of the current function or frame. The line of code being executed will be specially marked on the left.
`p expression`	Compute the value of the expression in the current context and print it out.
`Continue`	Continue execution and stop only when the next breakpoint is encountered.
`Step`	If the current line is a function call, enter the called function to continue debugging. Otherwise, execute the current line and stop at the next line of the current function.
`Next`	Execute the current line (whether it is a function call or not) and stop at the next line of the current function.
`Up`	Move the current frame to the old frame (the caller of the current frame) in the stack trace.
`Down`	Contrary to the up command, move the current frame to the new frame in the stack trace.

Figure 11.1 – Commonly used pdb commands

If you want to know more debugging commands, or learn more about using the `pdb` module, please go through the official documentation (https://docs.python.org/3/library/pdb.html).

Using an IDE to debug

Another way of debugging Python is to use a GUI-based IDE. In this example, we will work with the most commonly used Python IDE tool, **PyCharm** (`https://www.jetbrains.com/pycharm/`), to show the configuration method for debugging Rasa applications:

1. Let's begin with opening the **Run/Debug Configurations** interface.

2. Select **Run** > **Edit Configures.**

3. Click the + button in the upper-right corner, and select **Python** in the list that appears.

We will get the following configuration interface:

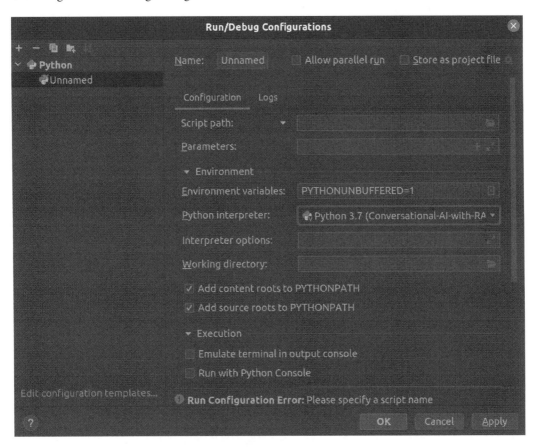

Figure 11.2 – Run/Debug Configurations interface for Python

Like using pdb, there are also two debugging options for an IDE. The first is module-based, and the second is file-based.

First, we will discuss the module-based approach. To do this, we need to make four changes to the default configuration shown in *Figure 11.2*:

1. First, we need to choose **Module name** as the running method. To open the selection list, click ▼ to the right of **Script path:** and select **Module name**.

2. Next, **Module name** is set to be rasa.

3. Next, **Parameters** should be set as the Rasa subcommand and parameters we need. In the command line, all of the Rasa command strings except for rasa are the parameters. For example, in the rasa train command, train is the parameter.

4. Finally, **Working directory** should be set as the rasa project path.

The following figure is an example of a complete module-based configuration:

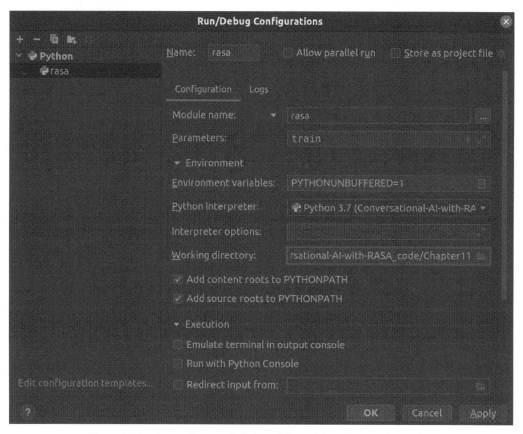

Figure 11.3 – A complete module-based Rasa debugging configuration

Another way to debug Rasa applications through an IDE is file-based. To do this, we need to make four changes to the default configuration shown in *Figure 11.2*:

1. First, we need to choose **Script path** as the running method, which is the default value. If it is not, click ▼ to the right of **Module name:** to open the selection list and select **Script path**.

2. Next, **Script path** is set to the file path of the entry module (`rasa.__main__`). We already discussed how to get the file path in the *Using the pdb module to debug* section.

3. Next, **Parameters** should be set as the Rasa subcommand and parameters we need. The settings for this part are the same as in the module-based debugging.

4. Finally, **Working directory** should be set as the `rasa` project path. The settings of this part are also completely consistent with module-based debugging.

The following figure is an example of a complete file-based configuration:

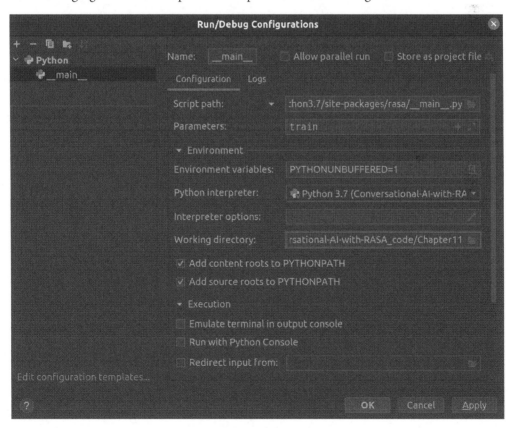

Figure 11.4 – A complete file-based Rasa debugging configuration

After this, we can use PyCharm to debug Rasa projects with breakpoints and the debugging dashboard.

Optimizing Rasa systems

For intent classification and entity extraction components based on machine learning, the learning rate and epoch settings are very important for the performance of this component. We can determine the adjustment direction (increase or decrease) of the learning rate and epoch by observing the loss curve.

In this example, we take the commonly used component in Rasa, DIETClassifier, as a way to illustrate how to adjust the settings to use **TensorBoard**, to visualize training and validation metrics. Here is an example of our Rasa configuration:

```
version: "2.0"
language: en
pipeline:
  - name: WhitespaceTokenizer
  - name: LanguageModelFeaturizer
    model_name: "bert"
    model_weights: "rasa/LaBSE"
  - name: RegexFeaturizer
  - name: DIETClassifier
    epochs: 100
    learning_rate: 0.001
    tensorboard_log_directory: ./log
policies:
  - name: MemoizationPolicy
  - name: TEDPolicy
    epochs: 100
  - name: RulePolicy
```

In the preceding example, we set the component to record the metrics changes during the training process to the specified directory (that is, ./log). After that, we use the rasa train command to train the model as usual. During and after training, we can observe the changes of these indicators through TensorBoard. You can start TensorBoard with the following command (in the Command Prompt or terminal):

```
tensorboard --logdir=./log
```

After the preceding command runs, users can access TensorBoard to observe the changes of various indicators by visiting `http://localhost:6006/`, as shown in the following figure:

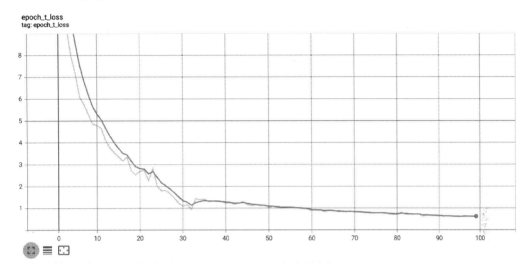

Figure 11.5 – Examining loss using TensorBoard

If the learning rate of the component is set too low, the weights in the network are updated very slightly at each step, so the training progress will be very slow (that is, the loss will decrease very slowly). However, if the learning rate is set too high, it may cause the strange behavior that the loss value continues to increase. You can use TensorBoard to check the loss to decide whether the current learning rate setting is reasonable, and if not, how to adjust it.

Let's discuss the epoch settings. If the epoch is set too low, the number of training iterations is too small, and the model is not fully trained (that is, the loss has not dropped to the lowest), so the model performs poorly. However, if the epoch is set too high, after the model finds the (local) optimal solution (that is, the loss has dropped to the lowest value and cannot continue to decrease), more training time will not be able to find a better solution, so more big epochs would be just a waste of time.

Understanding the community ecosystem of Rasa

Rasa only offers core infrastructure and does not offer additional tools to help developers build bots. Rasa focuses on solutions for NLU and dialogue management, however, to create a complete chatbot, we also need to work on data collection, data generation, data labeling, and so on. We can do this by writing scripts, but this is not friendly to developers.

There are some open source projects in the developer community that can help and may act as additional tools to work together with Rasa to build chatbots. We introduce some of those tools in the following subsections.

Data generation tool – Chatito

Chatito is a data generation tool that helps developers to generate data with the simple format of a **Domain-Specific Language** (**DSL**). A DSL is a computer language specially designed for a particular application domain. Using a DSL has many advantages, such as being much more expressive in their domain than general-purpose programming languages. Developers can use Chatito to rapidly generate training and testing data for natural language processing tasks such as **Named Entity Recognition** (**NER**), text classification, intent recognition, and so on.

A Chatito project consists of the following parts:

- An IDE for online editing
- A set of DSL protocols for natural language processing
- A DSL parser in pegjs format
- A generator implemented in TypeScript and the NPM package

The online editing IDE of Chatito is quite mature and supports grammar check and keyword highlighting, as shown here:

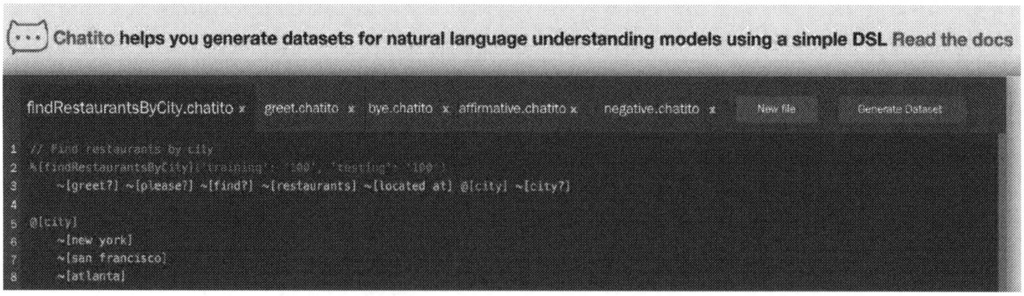

Figure 11.6 – Online IDE of Chatito

Chatito has a native adapter for Rasa that can generate NLU data in a compatible format. For more information about Chatito's DSL syntax and usage, please visit the GitHub repository: `https://github.com/rodrigopivi/Chatito`.

Data generation tool – Chatette

Chatette (`https://github.com/SimGus/Chatette`) is a tool similar to Chatito. It uses a DSL to generate data. The DSL used by Chatette is a superset and extension of Chatito's DSL. This means we can directly use Chatito templates in Chatette.

The main differences between Chatette and Chatito are as follows:

- Chatito is implemented in JavaScript, while Chatette is in Python.
- Chatito has multiple adapters that support different dialogue frameworks, while Chatette only supports Rasa.
- Chatette supports large-scale projects by allowing multiple file inputs, for instance.

In the following figure, we show an example of generating data from a Chatette DSL template:

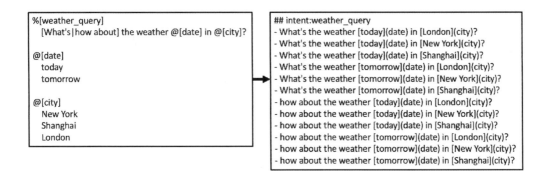

Figure 11.7 – From a Chatette DSL template to a dataset

In the preceding figure, the left side is the DSL template, and the right side is the NLU dataset generated by this template.

In this section, we showed you the powerful features of Chatette. For more information on Chatette's DSL syntax and usage, please visit the official Wiki (`https://github.com/SimGus/Chatette/wiki`).

Data labeling tool – Doccano

Doccano (`https://github.com/doccano/doccano`) is an open source, web-based, text labeling tool with a user-friendly and intuitive UI. It supports labeling for text classification, sequence labeling, and seq-to-seq labeling.

Some of Doccano's main features are as follows:

- Support for multi-user collaboration in labeling
- Support for multiple languages
- Support for labeling in mobile devices
- Support for emojis
- Support for dark mode UI
- Support for RESTful API

In the following figure, we show Doccano's named entity annotation function:

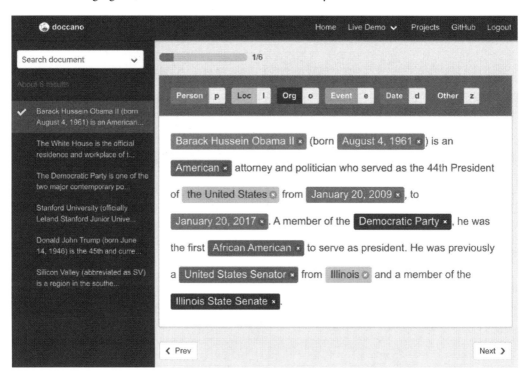

Figure 11.7 – The named entity annotation function of Doccano

From the preceding figure, we can see that Doccano's UI is professional and intuitive: different entities are distinguished by different colors, and it also supports shortcut keys (a single letter next to the entity name) to improve efficiency.

Next, we will show Doccano's text classification function, which can be used for intent classification:

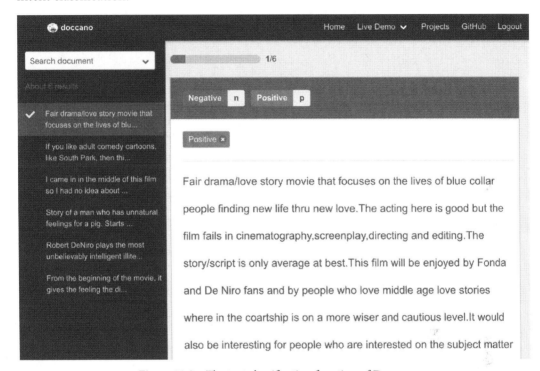

Figure 11.8 – The text classification function of Doccano

In this section, we showed you the rich features of Doccano. For detailed tutorials and documents on how to use Doccano, please visit `https://doccano.github.io/doccano/`.

Language-specific libraries

Although Rasa is a language-neutral framework, many components are language-specific or only support some languages. Rasa's support for different languages is not exactly the same. Developers from different parts of the world have contributed to building language-specific libraries to allow Rasa to better support their own languages.

One example is the **rasa_chinese** library (`https://github.com/howl-anderson/rasa_chinese`). It takes advantage of the flexibility of Rasa and adds components that specialize in processing Chinese (such as Chinese word segmentation, pre-training models, and so on). In addition to this, `rasa_chinese` supports connection to some well-known Chinese instant messaging applications, such as WeChat.

Summary

In this chapter, you learned how to debug a Rasa system and to optimize the performance of Rasa. You also learned about some excellent tools from the community that can help you.

When discussing how to debug a Rasa system, we introduced how to use the debugging information of the Rasa shell to deal with the problem of incorrect results run by Rasa. We then introduced how to use the `pdb` module and the IDE's debugging function to debug code errors.

When discussing how to optimize the performance of Rasa, we introduced how to use TensorBoard to observe the changes in metrics to determine how to adjust the learning rate and epoch settings.

Finally, we introduced you to some excellent tools from the Rasa community. By using these tools, your work efficiency can be greatly improved.

This is the last chapter of the book, so let's quickly review its main sections.

We started with an introduction to the architecture and underlying principles of the Rasa framework. Then we learned, in detail, how to quickly build various chat robots, such as task-based, FAQ, knowledge graph chat robots, and more. Finally, we gained knowledge about the best practices to adopt in the debugging and optimization of Rasa.

We hope that you got a lot out of this book. If you worked all the way through it, which is not easy, you should now consider yourself an expert in Rasa. All we can say is thank you very much for reading!

`Packt.com`

Subscribe to our online digital library for full access to over 7,000 books and videos, as well as industry leading tools to help you plan your personal development and advance your career. For more information, please visit our website.

Why subscribe?

- Spend less time learning and more time coding with practical eBooks and Videos from over 4,000 industry professionals

- Improve your learning with Skill Plans built especially for you

- Get a free eBook or video every month

- Fully searchable for easy access to vital information

- Copy and paste, print, and bookmark content

Did you know that Packt offers eBook versions of every book published, with PDF and ePub files available? You can upgrade to the eBook version at `packt.com` and as a print book customer, you are entitled to a discount on the eBook copy. Get in touch with us at `customercare@packtpub.com` for more details.

At `www.packt.com`, you can also read a collection of free technical articles, sign up for a range of free newsletters, and receive exclusive discounts and offers on Packt books and eBooks.

Other Books You May Enjoy

If you enjoyed this book, you may be interested in these other books by Packt:

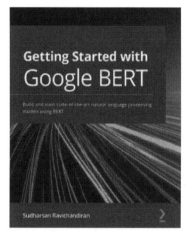

Getting Started with Google BERT

Sudharsan Ravichandiran

ISBN: 978-1-83882-159-3

- Understand the transformer model from the ground up
- Find out how BERT works and pre-train it using masked language model (MLM) and next sentence prediction (NSP) tasks
- Get hands-on with BERT by learning to generate contextual word and sentence embeddings
- Fine-tune BERT for downstream tasks
- Get to grips with ALBERT, RoBERTa, ELECTRA, and SpanBERT models
- Get the hang of the BERT models based on knowledge distillation
- Understand cross-lingual models such as XLM and XLM-R

Mastering spaCy

Duygu Altinok

ISBN: 978-1-80056-335-3

- Install spaCy, get started easily, and write your first Python script
- Understand core linguistic operations of spaCy
- Discover how to combine rule-based components with spaCy statistical models
- Become well-versed with named entity and keyword extraction
- Build your own ML pipelines using spaCy
- Apply all the knowledge you've gained to design a chatbot using spaCy

Packt is searching for authors like you

If you're interested in becoming an author for Packt, please visit `authors.packtpub.com` and apply today. We have worked with thousands of developers and tech professionals, just like you, to help them share their insight with the global tech community. You can make a general application, apply for a specific hot topic that we are recruiting an author for, or submit your own idea.

Share your thoughts

Now you've finished *Conversational AI with Rasa*, we'd love to hear your thoughts! Scan the QR code below to go straight to the Amazon review page for this book and share your feedback or leave a review on the site that you purchased it from.

https://packt.link/r/1801077053

Your review is important to us and the tech community and will help us make sure we're delivering excellent quality content.

Index

F

G

Made in the USA
Monee, IL
19 December 2021

86376659R00146